# Exploring the Christian Way

VERNON O. ELMORE

BROADMAN PRESS

Nashville, Tennessee

© Copyright 1978 Broadman Press

4281–34
ISBN: 0–8054–8134–6

Dewey Decimal Classification: 227.6
Subject headings: BIBLE. N. T. PHILIPPIANS//
COLOSSIANS//PHILEMON

Library of Congress Card Catalog Number: 77–073982
Printed in the United States of America

# Contents

# 1

## When the Saints Go Marching

COLOSSIANS 1:1–14

Confinement to a prison cell must have been an indescribable torment to an activist like Paul. However, it was providential for us. Otherwise he probably would never have taken the time from his preaching to put on paper his understanding of the Christian faith. In fact, messages from the jail are often amplified in their projection because of the circumstances of their production. John Bunyan, tinker turned thinker, employed his dozen years behind bars to write the potent Christian allegory *The Pilgrim's Progress.* The warped mind of Adolf Hitler wrote his *Mein Kampf* while he languished in prison. One of his victims, Dietrich Bonhoeffer, committed to paper his meditations while awaiting execution.

Do not expect to hear, however, the whimper of a condemned man in Paul's prison letters, but rather the call to Christian allegiance by a victor whose spirit circumstances could not quell. Corrie ten Boom's book *The Hiding Place* compels our attention because it exudes the smell of the Nazi concentration camp. We who sit on the comfortable sidelines should consider with great respect the reflections of those who have been through the fire.

### No Stage Divine

"An apostle by the will of God" is Paul's self-identification. This titan of Tarsus was stopped dead in his tracks on the Damascus road. He received marching orders which conflicted completely with his self-appointed mission to throttle the gospel witness. Christ changed him from a religious argonaut to a Spirit-filled apostle. His message, then, was the authentic word of a God-called man. Anyone who speaks for God other than by call is an apostle by presumption. He is what Erasmus characterized as a "stage divine." He is playing a role rather than fulfilling a commission.

The Lord is still recruiting shepherds for his flock. There is great concern among some religious groups about the shortage of young people entering the ministry. I have a notion that God will raise up from each religious entity as many ministers as that group deserves. Elton Trueblood has pointed out that a more appropriate term than *shepherd* to identify spiritual leaders today is *coach*. To a sports-oriented society, the word *coach* conveys understandable implications. The apostle Paul was a kind of Vince Lombardi to the Christians of his day. The book of Colossians is like a locker room pep talk at the halftime. The coach was saying, "All right, boys, you are doing a good job, but you've got to put out a little more. We're up against a tough team. We can't let down a minute or they will wipe us out."

## A Team Called Saints

The name of the team Coach Paul addressed in his letter was the "Colossians Saints." Sports fans are familiar with the New Orleans' Saints. They are so called because that city has become identified with a jazzed-up religious song, "When the Saints Go Marching In." There is also a team in your community called "Saints" and as a Christian, you are a team member. Every Christian is a saint! Paul would have been outraged by the reservation of that term for certain exceptionally pious persons, most of whom have been dead for decades. A saint is not a special Christian but any Christian. Saints do not sport halos and wear bed sheets. There are saints all over the place wearing dress suits, sport coats, blue jeans, housedresses, and evening gowns.

Mark Twain once accompanied a group of church people on a pilgrimage to the Holy Land. His comic observations of his fellow passengers were reported in a book called *Innocents Abroad.* He said that he got along very well with the professional clergy. As a matter of fact, Twain told his brother that he had an ambition as a youngster to become either a preacher or a river pilot. He gave up on being a preacher because he said he lacked the "necessary stock in trade; that is to say, religion." It was the pretentious religious amateurs on the ship who enraged Twain, including one unsmiling passenger whom he described as a "candidate for a vacancy in the Trinity."

People don't make the Christian team by some pious posture or even by their superlative character. Sainthood has to do with a relationship rather than an accomplishment. Saints are described as being "in Christ." What does that mean? The answer to that question is beyond human understanding. There are at least two suggestions which give me a small grasp on it. I sometimes say that I am in the Kiwanis Club. I mean by this that I belong to the club. I am a member. Saints in Christ belong to him. They have joined him and are members of his team. Beyond this, there is a genuine spiritual identification between Christ and the Christian. Christians are inseparable parts of one entity. The saint is one committed body and soul to Jesus Christ.

The Colossian saints were *in* Christ *at* Colossae. The saint has a special relationship to Christ and a spatial relationship to his environment. That environment is often hostile to the free expression of that sainthood. Therefore, thriving as a saint requires considerable determination and dedication. Paul implied that the most desired characteristic of a saint is faithfulness. He associated in his address "saints and faithful brethren." Probably not all of the saints in Colossae were faithful. In a typical church today, there is a relatively small minority who fit this description. Christ indicated that the highest commendation at the end of the game will be, "Well done, thou good and faithful servant." In the book of Revelation, Christ addressed saints living under stress with these words of encouragement: "Be thou faithful unto death, and I will give thee a crown of life" (Rev. 2:10). Faithful unto death not only means faithful until you die but also faithful even if you must die.

A sportscaster asked a Baylor football player why his team played with such determination and effort game after game.

The player replied, "Simply because Coach Teaff expects it of us, and we don't want to disappoint him." Christ expects his saints to be faithful, and the highest motivation is our love and respect for him. Here is the measure by which we determine how strenuously we are playing the game as one of the saints.

## Saints on the March

Abraham Lincoln was driven to frenzy by the do-nothing attitude of General McClellan. One biographer says that McClellan had built the most powerful army of its time but could not be persuaded to use it. He loved to prance on horseback in Washington parades and to posture before his troops, but he could not be made to fight. Churchill said of Kaiser Wilhelm that he wanted to be a Napoleon without fighting Napoleon's battles; the kaiser wanted victories without wars.

Paul praised the Colossian saints because they had gone on the march. They were not plaster saints assuming a Christian pose but were putting into practice the Christian ideals. They marched to the cadence of a threefold drum beat: faith, love, and hope. According to Paul in 1 Corinthians 13, these are the supreme marks of Christian maturity, the paramount expressions of true sainthood. First of all, the saint has faith in the Lord Jesus Christ. A man once said to me, "I believe in Christ with a little *c.*" He meant by this that he had reservations about the divine nature and mission of Christ. A feeble faith like this will sideline a saint. At best, he will march in place. Faith worthy of a compliment is a wholehearted commitment to Christ.

Chinese Gordon was a distinguished general in the British army. As a reward for his faithful military service, he was offered titles and other rewards. He refused all except one, a medal upon which had been imprinted his name and the many battles in which he had taken part. After General Gordon was killed at Khartoum, a search through his effects did not produce the medal. An entry in his diary finally disclosed what had happened to it. Once when a severe famine struck Manchester,

England, he had sent this medal to the city fathers with the request that it be melted down and the proceeds used to help feed the starving. In his diary, he wrote, "The last and only thing I have in this world that I value, I have given over to the Lord Jesus Christ." This was in the spirit of the sainthood which counts everything but refuse "for the excellency of the knowledge of Christ Jesus."

"Love to all the saints" is another sterling quality in saints who march. This love is not some cheap sentimentality that can be turned off like a hydrant. It is a deep, abiding spirit of good will and compassionate concern. The saint in action does not go around looking at his fellow Christians through dark glasses, disparaging and criticizing. His love always wants the best for the other person. It reaches out in helpfulness to others.

*Life* magazine once portrayed Dr. Denton Cooley, the famous heart surgeon, in conversation with one of his heart transplant patients. Dr. Cooley held in his hand a glass jar which contained the man's heart. The caption read: "The first man in history to look at his own heart." From time to time we need to look at our own hearts to be sure there is no hostility lingering there. We all must do a lot of praying to keep our hearts right.

The newspapers told sometime ago that the fish were dying in the Rhine River. It was discovered that about three hundred pounds of deadly insecticide had been dumped from a barge. Just a tiny bit of it was sufficient to kill the fish. Similarly, a little bit of hate goes a long way toward polluting our souls. On the other hand, love is a constructive force creating healthful Christian attitudes. It is said that everything King Midas touched turned to gold. The true Midas touch is love. Every relationship is enhanced, our outlook becomes more wholesome, and love releases spiritual energy to do good.

Hope is the third saintly trait. I like that story about the boy and his father who were planning a fishing trip for the next day. That evening as the father was putting his son to bed, the boy hugged his father's neck and said, "Daddy, thank you for tomorrow." The Christian hope bestows upon the saints the element of happy anticipation. The fact that we can look forward to the future makes the present more cheerful and our burdens lighter. My wife has the theory that a person should plan nice things ahead such as an outing or a dinner or a golf date. One of my joys is travel, and one of the pleasures of travel is the anticipation. By mapping out the trip in advance, you enjoy it both in advance and in actuality.

As Christians we have so much to look forward to. Our anticipation should be very keen. The hope of heaven and the blessings of eternal life encourage me at every turn. Freud once said, "The final victory belongs to the conqueror worm." No wonder he dreaded the thought of death. Hope, on the other hand, gives us a spiritual and psychological lift. The daily trials, the debilitation of old age, the reality of death all become more tolerable when we are buoyed by hope.

Once on the way to a cemetery, I overheard the pallbearers lamenting about how unprepared their friend had been for his death. A great burden, therefore, had fallen upon his wife. One of the men said, "This will never happen to me. I have made all the arrangements. I have purchased my cemetery plot and have a paid-up insurance policy." The preparation he had in mind is important but secondary. It is good to have an insurance policy paid up but better to have a hope "laid up," as Paul said. This gives the Christian an ultimate sense of security as he awaits tomorrow.

## Saints of Stature

Paul advised the Colossian saints, "I do not cease to pray for you." How would you like to have the apostle Paul praying for you? I am usually startled but genuinely pleased when people tell me they are praying for me. Saints may be mutually supportive in the fellowship of prayer. Paul revealed the objective of his prayers in behalf of the Colossians. He was praying that they would be quality Christians. Quality is not hard to tell. When I go to the store to buy a suit, the one I reach for is usually the most expensive one. That suit attracts my atten-

tion because quality shows. Manufacturers who pride themselves on the quality of their product may produce some
cheaper suits, but they usually do so under another label. Jesus
must be terribly embarrassed by the shoddy lives of some who
bear the label *Christian*.

The father of Frederick the Great of Prussia sought to
surround himself with giants. He had agents who scoured Europe to find men of unusual stature. They were conscripted
and sometimes even kidnapped to form his personal body-
guard. Paul prayed that the Colossian saints would grow up
to be spiritual giants. He even offered them a model of Christian
stature in Epaphras, "a faithful minister of Christ." It is often
helpful to take a good look at the best Christian we know
and emulate some of his qualities.

When I was a college student, George W. Truett came
to our state to preach at an evangelistic conference. I had read
his sermons and told his stories, but I wanted to see him in
person. Some of us ministerial students skipped a few classes
and drove to hear the great preacher. He was then near the
end of his ministry. I thought he had the most saintly look of
anyone I had ever seen. It was a tremendously inspiring experience. When we returned to campus, our Latin teacher, a
spunky and brilliant woman in her seventies, scolded us. "You
preacher boys are worshiping George Truett, and that's
wrong." No, we were not idolizing him but we were imitating
him. We could not have selected a better example by which
to mold our own character and ministry.

In 1960, my wife and I attended the Baptist World Alliance
in Rio de Janeiro. We had been in communication with a missionary friend there who made arrangements for us to stay
with a Brazilian doctor and his family. Before we left the States,
we wrote to the doctor and asked if there was anything we
could bring them from this country. He replied that one of
his daughters was small for her age. He had heard of a drug
available in America which sometimes stimulated growth. He
asked that we bring him a supply. Through our doctor we
were able to obtain the drug and carried it to Brazil.

Is there any special substance which stimulates spiritual growth? Paul said that the Colossians had heard the gospel and through it "knew the grace of God in truth." Grace is that special gift of God to his saints which enables them to grow toward maturity. In 2 Peter 3:18, we have the admonition, "grow in grace." The more receptive we are to the grace of God in our lives, the more we grow in Christlikeness. God can't bestow grace upon us unless we offer him an empty vessel. Paul suggested some practical ways in which we can absorb more of God's grace.

First of all, Paul prayed that the Colossians might have a worthy walk. In other words, their lives were to be sincerely dedicated to Christ. God is not going to pour his grace into a cesspool. I feel that God exercises a very strict economy in respect to his grace, investing only where it draws dividends. The Christian who is conscientiously living for Jesus is the one who will be the object of his largess. Paul Dietzel, a Christian football coach, once declared, "I want to take out of my life everything not pleasing to Christ." A decision like that is an initial step on the road to Christian maturity.

Living for Jesus is not simply a negative matter, however, for Paul continued to emphasize "good works" as an ingredient in the Christian commitment. Simeon Stylites, a fifth-century ascetic, sat on a tall, stone pillar for thirty years thinking that thereby he was serving Jesus. Robert Benchley, the humorist, used to say, "I do my work sitting down. That's where I shine." Some Christians do their work for Jesus sitting in a church pew on Sunday morning and feeling that they have fulfilled their calling thereby. Christ didn't intend for his saints to be bench warmers but to get in the game. A positive involvement in Christian service is a necessary condition for receiving more grace.

Wisdom and spiritual understanding also release grace into our lives. Peter's encouragement was to "grow in grace, and in the knowledge of our Lord and Saviour Jesus Christ" (2 Pet. 3:18). An essential to acquiring spiritual understanding is the study of the Bible and Christian literature. Francis Asbury, the famous Methodist bishop of the eighteenth century, encouraged every Methodist to be a reader. He declared, "It cannot be that the people should grow in grace unless they give themselves to reading. A reading people will always be a knowing people."

How can I tell if I am growing in grace? In verse 11, Paul named three positive results of Christian growth. They are like litmus paper in that they will immediately reflect the presence or absence of grace. Lay your own life alongside these three attributes, and you can get an idea of your own saintly stature. The three attributes are patience, long-suffering, and joy. Patience means the ability to endure for Christ and let him get glory from whatever happens to you. Long-suffering means the ability to treat others with kindness and consideration no matter how insufferable they may be. Joy is the deep down happiness and peace that persists through all of life's circumstances. So size yourself up by these three traits and determine how big you are as a Christian.

## Thankful Saints

During World War II, a fighter pilot bailed out into occupied France. His life was saved by the courageous French people who sheltered him and helped him escape. After the war was over, the pilot took all the money he could scrape together and went back to Normandy to look for the people who had helped him. Of the twenty people who had risked their lives for him, he found nineteen. One had been killed in the final fighting. The pilot bought food and clothing which these people sorely needed and did everything he possibly could to show them his gratitude for saving his life.

Saints are thankful also to the heavenly Father who loved us and gave his Son to die for us. Saints were once sinners whom God has taken into his own family and made them heirs of his blessings. Saints were once slaves to sin but have been delivered from the power of darkness. Saints were once sentenced to eternal damnation but have been forgiven by his grace.

Gratitude is the motivation for the saint's loyalty to Christ and for whatever sacrifices he makes in the course of his spiritual career. It is remarkable to observe in Paul's writings how often he paused to break into an exclamation of thanksgiving. In spite of all he suffered for the cause of Christ in the course of his missionary travels, his prevailing disposition was one of gratitude. This hymn of praise is all the more thrilling because it was conceived and first sung in a Roman prison cell.

Lyman Abbott succeeded Henry Ward Beecher in 1890 as pastor of the Plymouth Church in Brooklyn. He was a great friend of Beecher and loved him dearly. Beecher was the subject of a great deal of slander and abuse. Abbott in his autobiography says, "I wanted to stand where some of the shots aimed at him would strike me." This reminds us of the great devotion of Paul to Jesus Christ which led him to rejoice in his suffering for Christ's sake.

Herbert Hoover was one of the most vilified and maligned presidents in the history of our nation because the Great Depression began during his administration. He did not seem to become cynical or bitter. He went on serving his country to the end, maintaining his dignity and serenity. His wife once explained it like this: "Bert can take it better than most people because he has deeply ingrained in him the Quaker feeling that nothing matters if you are right with God."

Here, then, is the secret of a well-adjusted life, the life of a saint who can take adversity and put up with human perversity. The saint is right with God through Christ and, therefore, is right with himself and his fellowman. This allows him the freedom to march, unshackled by guilt and unintimidated by fear. He is set at liberty to be man as God meant him to be.

# 2

## A Secret God Couldn't Keep

COLOSSIANS 1:15–23,27–29

We all know how difficult it is to keep a secret. It sprouts wings and comes fluttering out of our mouth before we know it. God has a secret locked up in his heart which demanded telling. He couldn't just blurt it out because no one would have believed it. A secret so enormous in its implications deserved and demanded a very special medium of communication. Jesus Christ was that divine messenger who conveyed to mankind truth about God and the world which man could never have discovered if he searched a million years. Any ideas that man conceives about ultimate origins are nothing but theories which can never be proved. The testimony of fact must come from the Originator himself.

### Footprints of God

It is said that one-fifth of the world's population watched the television broadcast of the first man setting foot on the moon. This was an incredible achievement which is still difficult to believe. Something even more astonishing happened, however, when God set foot on earth. Christ's coming was a divine visitation. Just as Armstrong and Aldrin planted the American flag on the moon, God raised his standard on the earth. It was a cross. For thirty-three years God in Christ left footprints on this planet. They say that the footprints of the astronauts will last a million years on the moon. After two thousand years, the footprints of Christ are just as fresh as the day of his visitation. The impact of his presence is still felt in the souls of men.

I was startled by a close-up view of Christ's face in the recent television production about the life of Christ. Christ had brilliant blue eyes. Christ was a Semite in his physical ancestry, and blue eyes were very unlikely. Paul insisted that there are no such inconsistencies in the image of God in Christ. Jesus was God materialized before our eyes.

Shortly before the turn of the century, a young man from Ohio homesteaded in the wilderness of the Dakotas. He built himself a sod house, and the Indians were his only neighbors. In desperation for companionship, he wrote a lonely hearts organization requesting correspondence with some young lady. Down in the hills of southern Missouri, a newspaper man saw that plea and as a kind of joke answered it in the name of his cousin. Without her knowing it, he carried on correspondence for some time with the lonely man in the Dakotas. When the young lady found out about it, she was embarrassed and enraged. She finally consented to read the letters, and as the homesteader seemed to be a man of integrity, she then took up the correspondence. After some time, she received a letter announcing that he was coming to see her. One day, the man who had simply been a name, a phantom figure, arrived and introduced himself. The young people fell in love and returned to the sod house together. They had a long and happy marriage. I know because they were my uncle and aunt.

Before Christ came into the world, God was real enough but seemed so distant, so intangible, and ill-defined. In Jesus, God stepped off the train, so to speak, and walked down main street for every eye to see and for every person to know. Jesus came saying, "He that hath seen me hath seen the Father" (John 14:9).

When Paul said that Jesus was the image of the invisible God, he did not mean that Jesus was like God. He meant that Jesus was God.

For fifteen years in San Antonio, we were neighbors with identical twins whose houses were side by side. They told me of an amusing mix-up which occurred shortly after they were married. One of the brothers took his wife to a beach resort for a brief vacation. When they returned, the other brother and his wife went to the same resort. The landlady was very bewildered and upset. One day she called the wife aside and confidentially told her that her husband had been there the week before with another woman.

Christ was identical with God not only in the sense of similarity but also in sameness. Christ and God are not twin beings but one and the same. In Christ dwelt all "fulness" (v. 19). In other words, nothing of God was missing in Christ. Christ, then, was the perfect revelation of God. He was God in person. God was no longer a mystery guest; in Christ, God stood up and identified himself. In Christ, God is someone whom we can recognize, call by name, and get to know on a personal basis.

## The Whole World in His Hands

Can you imagine a time before time when there was nothing but God, no earth, no stars, no space? Before all the mass, immensity, and minutiae of creation, Christ was. He is as old as God for he is God. He is the fountain of existence, the author of all that is. He created all creation. He authored all authority. He systematized all systems. He ordained all orbits. He manufactured all matter. He is as superior to his creation as the artist to his canvas or the potter to his vessel.

The learned minds do not often grapple with ultimate origins. They prefer to theorize about intermediate phenomena such as whether the earth flew out of the sun or whether the planets were compacted out of space particles. The question of questions is not often on their lips: Where did space come from? Has it always been? The Christian answer is that everything other than God was created out of nothing by God. We either believe that matter was created or that it is eternal. Such thoughts send our minds spinning. Paul said that in Christ, at last, the secret has been let out. Christ is the originator and the coordinator of all existence. Christ brought everything into being and keeps it in tact.

Suddenly we find ourselves with a bigger image of Christ than we sometimes entertain. Too often we look at Christ through the wrong end of a telescope. He is no Lilliputian we can mock and maul and do with as we please. He is not a Jolly Green Giant who looks upon all our foibles with a wink and a ho! ho! ho! He is none other than the Maker and Master of all that is.

## Head of the Corporation

Paul moved from an illimitable universe in his consideration of Christ's preeminence to a much more confined and defined entity called the church. Paul spoke of the church as a body, a corporation. Christ's authority over the corporation is as complete as that of the head over the body. Christians are a people who live under the lordship of Christ. In all of creation there is only one thing which can disobey Christ. It is not the elements, for the winds and waves heed his command. It is not demons, for they fled into the swine at his words and were hurled into the sea. It is not the trees, for Christ cursed the fruitless fig, and it bore fruit no more. It is not disease, for Christ cured the incurable and healed the hopeless. Not even death could disobey him, for he called a corpse from the tomb. There is only one who can disobey him, and that is man upon whom he exhausted his creative genius.

In all of his lovely creation, God wanted something which could love him in return. He bestowed upon man an element of deity itself. Never does man more nearly approximate deity than in the experience of love. This was the crowning act of God's ingenuity. There was always the possibility that man's love could become inverted, however, and rather than loving God, entertain an obsessive affection for himself. This is basically what sin is, loving self more than loving God.

Man's sin, then, is an alienation of affection. Rather than being lovers of God, we become enemies. Rather than being obedient to his authority, we become rebels intent upon doing our own thing. In one further act of love, God sought to reclaim the love of man. This he did in the redemptive death of Christ on the cross. Christ stepped down from the throne of the universe where he presided over the multiplied millions of stars to submit himself to the ridicule and abuse of spiteful humanity.

At any moment Christ could have hurled the earth into the sun or thrown the stars into confusion so that the earth would have convulsed in a spasm of death. Instead, he suffered in the flesh all the agonies of which the human body is capable, that body he designed with such exquisite sensitivity. It was no less than this Lord of the universe that the brutal Roman soldiers ridiculed and roasted with their scathing scorn as he hung on the middle cross. He might have flung the nails from his hands and turned the cross into a throne and the thorn crown into a jewel-studded diadem. He chose to hang there in ignominy not because he was powerless, but because he was possessed by a love of which only God is capable.

Why did he do so? Paul said, "All things were created by him, and for him." Everything, including people, belongs to Jesus. He died on the cross to reclaim that which was his. By the power of the cross, man, alienated by sin, is drawn to the Savior and incorporated into his body, under his lordship. The Creator thus becomes the re-creator. "If any man be in Christ, he is a new creature" (2 Cor. 5:17).

## A Changed Picture

I saw an advertisement in a magazine which contained two contrasting pictures. The first was that of a busy street in a downtown business section. The street was cluttered with telephone poles, wires, and cables, signs of various sizes protruding from the fronts of businesses. The second picture was an architectural drawing of the same scene with all the clutter removed. Wires and cables had evidently been placed underground. Gone were the motley signs. The street now had a simplicity and dignity utterly lacking in the picture from life.

There is potential beauty in every life. Our lives tend to become cluttered with attitudes and actions that detract from our beauty and deprive us of dignity and sap our spiritual energy. God, the great architect, longs to get hold of our lives and reshape us into the beautiful people he intended us to be. Change comes very painfully, however, because we have a built-in resistance. It is even difficult to admit that we need any change. The hackles rise on the back of our neck when someone implies that something is amiss in our character or behavior. Frequently, we retaliate with our own six shooters of criticism and personal fury.

Change is difficult because it strikes deep into our personalities. We are born into this world with certain ancestral patterns bred into us. Change means we have to dig around in the very roots of our being. This can be very upsetting and traumatic.

Change is difficult because it demands getting out of old familiar ruts and breaking new paths for ourselves. We have grown accustomed to facing life in a certain way. It is not a simple matter to alter the pattern. Some people say, "If I had my life to live over, I'd do differently." Chances are that if you came with the same essential makeup and in a similar environment, you would do about the same. Flip Wilson says, "If I could live my life over, I wouldn't have the strength."

The other day I read that one hundred thousand husbands abandon their families every year. These husbands plan to get away and live a different life. An organization which traces these men says that usually they are not difficult to find. In the new community they follow the same routines. We have a hard time escaping ourselves. This is why we need Jesus and his spiritual power to bring off that change. Paul could testify to the dramatic alteration of his life as a result of encountering Jesus. The woman at the well was a barren desert, and Jesus transformed her into a fruitful oasis. Zacchaeus was changed from a money-grubbing tightwad to a generous-hearted steward.

Many years ago, an armed robbery occurred at a photographic store in San Antonio. Several days later a woman in my church came to me and told me in confidence that her husband had committed the crime. He had fled the city, leaving his family to fend for themselves. A few months later, she returned to tell me that her husband was back and was holed up at home. Not even the children knew he was there. I wanted to go to the home and talk with him, but she was afraid for

me to do so. She said, "He's got an arsenal down there." She
did communicate to him my request that he come to see me.

In a couple of days the husband appeared at my office.
He was frightened, remorseful, and didn't know what to do.
I took him to the district attorney's office where he surrendered
himself. Released on bail, he returned to his old job and began
repaying the money he had taken. One day I took the man
to visit with the owner, a Baptist deacon. He apologized for
his wrong, and the deacon prayed for him. Later the grand
jury returned a "No Bill" in view of his conscientious efforts
at restitution.

I went to see this man at his home and explained that
someone else wanted also to forgive him. The same day that
the grand jury gave him a "No Bill," Jesus washed his sins
away. The next Sunday he and his son walked down the aisle
and publicly confessed Christ. Eagerly he sought ways to serve
Christ in his church and community. He died several years
later at a relatively young age. When I preached his funeral,
I rejoiced to remember that day when Jesus gave him a "No
Bill." This man's story has fortified for me the conviction of
the power of Jesus Christ to change lives.

### The Secret God Wants Everyone to Know

God has let the whole world in on the biggest and best
kept secret of all time. Humanity had played a guessing game
until the coming of Jesus. The various religions were efforts
to probe the secret about how man could find peace with God.
The matter still remained a deep dark mystery. The great
prophets had been given some preliminary insights, but it remained for Jesus to break the seal of the envelope of God's
will and purpose for man. The secret of secrets is this: Salvation
is available to the whole world through Jesus Christ. Christ is
God's answer to the destructive power of sin and Satan for
everyone. The gospel is God's secret and superweapon to counteract the forces of evil.

A few years ago I was invited, along with some other citi-
zens, to fly as a guest of the military to El Paso to visit the

missile proving grounds. We were given a special demonstration of the effectivemess of our missile program and assured by the generals that our American shores are safe. I am grateful for the strong military defenses of our country. I am sensitive to the fact, however, that I am under attack daily by sinister forces intent upon my destruction. Who shall deliver me from these malignant powers whose corruptive ability is far greater than that of Communism or other national foes? Paul shares the secret with us, "Christ in you, the hope of glory" (v. 27).

Augustine bore powerful testimony in his *Confessions* of the effectiveness of the gospel to enable man to escape the ravages of sin. He was a sensual man intent upon tasting the worldly delight of Rome. He was also a man with a conscience plagued by a sense of futility and guilt. So he left his home in Africa for Rome.

One day Augustine took refuge in his garden so he could examine his life. Suddenly, he heard the singsong voice of a child saying, "Take it and read it." Over and over the phrase was repeated. He rushed to where he had left a copy of the Bible open at the epistle to the Romans. He took it up and read, "Not in revelling and drunkenness, not in chambering and wantonness, not in strife and jealousy. But put ye on the Lord Jesus Christ, and make no provisions for the flesh, to regard the lusts thereof" (Rom. 13:13).[1] Augustine said that he had no wish to read any more and no need to do so. "It was as though the light of confidence flooded into my heart and all the darkness and doubt was dispelled." He returned to Africa and devoted his life to the service of Christ and became the famous Bishop of Hippo. The splendor of God began to shine from his life the moment he let Christ in.

A few years ago, a newly converted entertainer wrote the popular song, "It Is No Secret What God Can Do." Indeed, the secret is out. The mystery has been resolved. Millions of lives redeemed by the grace of the Lord Jesus Christ bear witness to the power of Christ to transform and reclaim people of all walks for God. The recent born-again testimonies of people like President Jimmy Carter, Charles Colson, and Eldridge

Cleaver have impressed the nation with the fact that there is something dynamically life-changing about the gospel.

## A Secret to Be Shared

As Christians we are God's secret agents. I mean that we are the ones to share with the world this marvelous secret. God is counting on us to carry the good news to the ends of the earth. Had you ever thought how frustrating, how agonizing, it must be to the heavenly Father that so many people live and die without ever knowing of his love in Christ?

Alexander Graham Bell was a teacher of the deaf by profession. His grandfather and father had developed a system for teaching the deaf to speak by the use of phonic symbols. It was as a by-product of his speech studies that Bell conceived the telephone. His invention came when he was still a very young man. He had fallen in love with and married one of his deaf pupils. He taught her to read lips and to speak so that many did not recognize that she was deaf when they met her. There was one great regret of his life, however, which he communicated to his wife in a letter: "I only wish, Darling, that you could hear my instrument."

"How shall they hear without a preacher?" Paul asked (see Rom. 10:14). He indicated in verse 29 the personal effort and agony he expended in seeking to bear the words of life to the world. I fear that many of us want people to be saved without any strenuous effort on our part. We build nice churches, have pews with soft cushions, cultured preachers, and robed choirs thinking that people should delight to flock into our churches.

The fact is that people are saved when Christians care enough to agonize in prayer and go in person to share the secret. Herein lies one of the problems. So few seem willing to pay the price. In many instances in our churches, we have programmed and promoted and organized, but we have not agonized. Consequently, the gospel is one of the best kept secrets in history. I would imagine that 75 percent of the American people have no more than a vague notion of what Christianity is all about. They know something about churchianity but not much about Christianity.

Queen Elizabeth I died March 24, 1603, at three o'clock in the morning. As soon as it was light, Sir Robert Carey stole out of the palace grounds and galloped off for Edinburgh. He rode 397 miles in less than 60 hours and arrived on his last panting relay in the courtyard of Holyrood Palace. Weary as he was, he asked to be taken into the presence of James VI of Scotland. He was the first to announce to him that he was now king of England, as well.

There are so many things that we are eager to tell. If somebody wins a popcorn popper in a chain store drawing, he can't wait to share the news. A bit of scurrilous gossip will be all over town in twenty minutes. The news of a new grandchild will be told by telephone and flashing photographs.

On VE Day, I was listening to a reporter who excitedly said that this is the greatest news ever heard. It was, indeed, good news that the war in Europe was over. The best news, however, is that Jesus Christ died for the sins of the world. This is a message that needs to be told as quickly as possible to every person in the world.

*Notes*

1. The American Standard Version of the Bible (New York: Thomas Nelson and Sons, 1901).

# 3

## Roots

COLOSSIANS 2:6–19*a*

Alex Haley has made an intensive search into his ancestry and incorporated his fascinating story into a book called *Roots*. Millions of people saw its serialization on television, and as a result there has been an increased interest in genealogy. People are leafing through musty records, querying aged relatives, and probing archives in quest of their predecessors. As Christians, we have a common heritage. Paul's writings remind us that we are rooted in Christ Jesus. We trace our spiritual heritage to Christ and his grace.

### Proud of Our Ancestry

I heard about a fellow who was studying his family tree and discovered that one of his ancestors had died in the electric chair. He made a notation alongside the name in his genealogical chart, "occupied the chair of applied electricity in one of our better known institutions." Christians do not need to make any apology concerning our illustrious predecessor. Indeed, Jesus died a common criminal's death and was buried in a borrowed tomb, but there was not one shameful smudge on his record. His innocent death on the cross was the price of our redemption. The trial of our spiritual ancestry leads up a steep path to a place called Golgotha. At the foot of the cross we discover the roots of Christian life and hope.

Alex Haley is obviously proud of the fact that he can trace his ancestry back to African royalty. The blood of heaven's royalty flows in our veins, so to speak. A cherished song declares, "I'm a child of the King." Many people display on their walls a family heraldic shield, giving evidence that somewhere in their background there was royalty. Paul said that it is not

25

enough to bear the name of Christ and pride ourselves upon
our royal descendency. He issued the instruction, "Walk ye
in him" (v. 6). The very best evidence of our spiritual ancestry
is a life consistent with his teaching and example.

The Duke of Windsor wrote his autobiography telling of
his early life as the Prince of Wales and his renunciation of
the throne of England. He said that his father, the king, often
remonstrated him, "Remember your position and who you
are." In other words, his behavior was to be consistent with
his identity as a child of the king. Friedrick Nietzsche once
hurled a stinging challenge at Christians. This atheistic philosopher, who spawned some of the Nazi ideas, said, "You Christians must look more redeemed if you expect me to believe
in your Redeemer."

Gandhi was often quoted as saying that he would be a
Christian if it weren't for Christians. His exposure to Christianity was largely of an institutionalized rather than personalized
form. On at least one occasion, however, he saw Christianity
in action. When he was wounded by a hostile mob, a missionary
family took him in and cared for him until he was able to
continue his peaceful revolution.

I agree with the statement that "we need less publicity
on how to stay young and more on how to grow up." The
secret of spiritual maturity Paul suggested is to sink our roots
deeper and deeper into Christ and his teachings. Growth is
always the result of proper nourishment. I once read in "Believe It or Not" about a boy who consumed nothing but soda
pop. There are Christians who are also on soda pop diets. The
only thing that turns them on, perhaps, is a service where
there is a lot of emotionalism or where the preacher is entertaining. They may become mesmerized by a popular religious
personality on television. They would drive a hundred miles
to get in on a great crusade but can't find the time or incentive
to engage in a serious study of the Bible. Religion is so often
a tune they pat their foot to rather than an intimate personal
walk with Jesus.

## Watch Out for the Isms

R. G. Lee says there are a lot of "isms that should be wasms." Mooneyism is the current religious fad which is making the headlines. You can be sure that there will be others to succeed it in the years ahead. In almost every generation some charismatic figure looms on the scene with his or her own individualized interpretation of Christianity and, surprisingly enough, collects a following. This suggests that many Christians are not being well grounded in the faith and that there are always those who become fascinated with anything new. The same thing was true in Paul's day, for Colossians was written largely to counteract a heretical version of Christianity called Gnosticism.

How are we to judge the validity of any particular religious movement? Primarily by what it has to say about Jesus. Some of the Gnostics said that Jesus was not divine. Others claimed that he was not really a human when on earth. There are those today who teach that Jesus is not equal with God. Others say that he was purely human. The biblical revelation of Jesus should always be the criterion by which the genuineness of any teaching is first of all tested.

There are competing philosophies which challenge Christianity in their efforts to claim the allegiance of humanity. Communism is the most potent of these ideologies and is sweeping through the world like a vacuum cleaner gathering up whole nations under its sway. Materialism is not so readily identified as a rival of Christianity, but it is the working philosophy of millions. An industrial firm has as its slogan, "Better Things for Better Living." A better living is the summum bonum for many people. It is their goal and life ambition. Of course, in order to have a better living they must have better things. Better cars, better houses, better clothes, better washing machines, these become the gods to which they devote their existence.

Jesus said, "I am come that they might have life, and that

they might have it more abundantly" (John 10:10). Jesus is the root source of life that is replete with the things that really matter. Eldridge Cleaver had to find this out the hard way. He was a fiery black activist who jumped bail on an indictment stemming from a shootout between police and Black Panther Party members. He fled the United States, was welcomed in Cuba, was given red carpet treatment in Communist countries. Suddenly, he returned to the United States saying, "I'd rather be in jail in the United States than free in any other country of the world."

Cleaver's political idols had been Engels, Marx, Castro, and Mao. As he visited the countries where their ideas were practiced, he sensed the emptiness and futility of it all. That was when he turned to Jesus in a heartfelt conversion experience. He devotes his time now to witnessing for Christ. Cleaver was asked in an interview how he was handling the problem of spiritual growth and maturity. He replied that he couldn't think of anything more important to a Christian than reading the Bible. "Without the Bible, what would there be?" In other words, the Christian needs to keep close to his roots.

## Completeness in Christ

A Sunday School teacher asked one of her pupils, "Who made you?"

The little boy replied, "I'm not done yet." I can appreciate the feeling of that lad. I don't think I'm done yet, either. I really don't know how far along in the process of being built I am. Sometimes I feel like a house under construction, the foundation has been laid, the rough framework is up, and the roof is on. The finish work has yet to be done. Patiently and skillfully the great Carpenter labors on with what little help I can give him. Almost every day vandals come along and undo some of his handiwork, so he has to start all over again.

Paul said, "Ye are complete in him" (v. 10). Whatever hope I have of becoming a whole person is in my relation to Jesus Christ. Literally, Paul was saying, "He fills you full." In the previous verse he declared, "For in him dwelleth all the fullness

of the Godhead bodily." There is nothing missing of God in
Jesus Christ. He is full of God and when we accept Christ,
he pours some of his fullness into our lives. We do not become
gods, but we participate in his nature and characteristics. This
enables us to become the kind of persons God intended us
to be. In other words, Christ finishes the work of making us
after God's pattern or blueprint. He completes us.

A man in my church purchased a color TV kit intending
to build his own set. He spent five hours just inventorying
the parts. Suppose someone came into his house and stole some
of the strategic parts and he was not able to find replacements.
That cold, colorless, silent set would haunt him and fill him
with frustration every time he looked at it. God must also be
dismayed at the sight of millions of people who are unfinished.
They have a life of a kind and find some meaning in their
existence, but some vital parts are missing which only Christ
can provide. They are only partial selves living a partial life.
They are just rough versions of what God intended them to
be.

A friend of mine recently surprised his aged parents with
a generous act. Life has been kind to him, and he has acquired
wealth. The house in which his parents lived had grown old
along with them. While they were away on a brief vacation,
he took a crew of carpenters to the house, tore out the walls,
moved partitions, laid carpets, put in new fixtures, replaced
the worn out furniture, and completely modernized the house.
When the parents returned, they were astonished and hardly
recognized their old house. When Christ comes into our lives,
he refurbishes them. The old shell is still there, but we are
all new on the inside. He renews us with life from above.

## Our Best Friend

Henry Ford once asked a man with whom he was having
lunch, "Who is your best friend?" When the man was hesitant
in his answer, Ford said, "I can tell you who your best friend
is." With that he began to write on the tablecloth the sentence:
"Your best friend is he who brings out the best that is within

you." By that definition, Jesus is certainly our best friend. He subdues and helps eliminate our inferior qualities and elicits from us our highest potential as a person.

Sin and death are the ancestral curses passed along from one generation to another. We all participate in the same kind of spiritual rebellion that characterized our predecessors, beginning with Adam and Eve. The expression "dead in sin" not only identifies the agent of our spiritual death but also the realm in which we exist without Christ. It is the realm of spiritual desolation and darkness. Sin enters our souls in the cemetery of hopelessness. It is from this spiritual graveyard that Christ raises us when we accept him as Savior.

The spiritually dead are unresponsive to God and his will. When God speaks, they do not hear, or if they hear, they do not heed. They are spiritually inert. A lonely, febbleminded man lived with his mother. When she died in the home, he propped her body in a chair and kept her there several days before anyone else knew she was dead. He talked to her and pretended that she was alive. God is no more successful in communicating with the spiritually dead.

The dead in sin are spiritually impotent. What a frustration to dash out to your car when you are almost late to an appointment, turn the key in the ignition and nothing happens. The battery has gone dead. It has lost its charge. This symbolizes the spiritual condition of the spiritually dead. They are like a battery with a dead cell. They can't even take a charge. The sinner can get charged up about a lot of things such as his work, a football game, a vacation trip, but we will never see him excited about attending church or studying the Bible or witnessing for Christ. In fact, it is impossible for him to experience any lasting emotions in these areas for he is spiritually a corpse.

The dead in sin are spiritually useless. In the aftermath of Hurricane Celia, our home was without electricity for two weeks. The line which ran from our house to the light pole had been torn loose. We had a house full of electrical gadgets but not one of them working. We had electric lights but had to burn candles. We longed for ice but the refrigerator sat mute. We were cut off from the source of power. Every person has a tremendous potential for service to God, but life is really useless until it is connected to him through Christ.

The dead in sin are spiritually hopeless as far as the future is concerned. They have nothing to look forward to except aggravated tragedy. The *Family Weekly* contained a story entitled, "What Death Row Has Taught Me About Living." It was written by a man who had existed in San Quentin's death row for nearly seven and a half years. On the occasional instances when he was permitted outside his cell, the officers escorting him would often shout to the other prisoners, "Move aside, dead man coming!" The sinner lives on spiritual death row. He awaits only the ultimate disaster of his transference by physical death to that eternal death row called hell.

Jesus Christ, our dearest friend, visits that cemetery in which lost souls are moldering and calls them to life. Paul said that, first of all, those sins which caused the sentence of death are forgiven (v. 13). Sin is primarily an offense against God. God cannot be true to his own character and permit sin to go unjudged. Upon the cross, Jesus bore our offense and paid our penalty. Thus, God is at liberty to forgive our sins. The sinner who accepts Christ is restored to God's favor.

The expression, "blotting out the handwriting of ordinances that was against us" (v. 14), is Paul's beautiful and picturesque way of describing what happens to our sin and guilt through Christ. The ink used in ancient times had no acid content and did not etch itself into the paper. It could be easily sponged away and the paper reused. The word translated "blotting out" was employed to describe this process. All the record of our sin is wiped away when Christ saves us. It is as though we had never sinned once in our life.

Our sin debt was paid in the death of Christ. It was "nailed to the cross." Sometime ago, Billy Graham received a ticket for a minor traffic violation. When Mr. Graham appeared in traffic court, the judge recognized the famous evangelist whom he admired greatly. In order to be true to his responsibility as a judge, it was necessary for him to exact a fine upon Mr. Graham. Justice had to be done. But then the judge stepped down from the bench and, out of his friendship for Mr. Graham, paid the fine himself.

When Jesus Christ died on the cross, God stepped down from his seat of judgment to pay off our sin debt. In this way, God disarmed all of those spiritual foes bent upon our destruction. When we accept Christ, we are no longer at the mercy of the malignant spiritual powers that have sought to thwart God's plan for our lives. On the cross Christ triumphed over Satan and his cohorts. We are free at last to live by God's will.

When I was called as a young man to the pastorate of a church in San Antonio, Texas, a deacon of financial means took me to the bank of which he was a director and introduced me to its officers. As I opened an account with my meager funds, the deacon said to the personnel, "If my pastor inadvertently writes a check without having sufficient funds to cover it, you charge it to my account." I was overwhelmed by this generosity. Jesus Christ not only takes care of our past sin debts but also our future ones. They are all covered by his blood. Does this mean we should live presumptuously? I would have been a real scoundrel if I had taken advantage of my deacon's generosity and written checks carelessly. Can I treat Christ with any less consideration in view of his grace exhibited to me at Calvary?

## Revised Versions

It is interesting to observe that if a unique and entertaining program has been introduced on television, the very next season there will be a flock of imitations, none of which are as good as the original. Christianity was hardly off the ground when imitators appeared on the scene. In some instances, elements of Christian teaching were mixed with the peculiar notions of an individual or group, and this new dogma became a rival for the real thing. Paul strongly warned the Colossians about these teachings which were shadowy misrepresentations

of the truth. Vance Havner has issued a sage bit of advice
for modern Christians: "Watch out for people who think they
have seen visions when they've only had nightmares."

There seem to be so many versions of Christianity that
people are frequently confused when searching for the real
thing. Many of these versions are actually revised versions and
have little association with genuine Christianity. There is a
distressing tendency toward religious fadism so that almost any
aberration of the Christian faith can elicit a following. Remember, there is one final test of the validity of any such version:
What does it say about Jesus? Does it belittle, distort, supercede,
or contradict the biblical revelation of Jesus? There are instances in which Jesus is imprisoned in a ritual or salvation is
made conditional upon some act of man rather than simply
the grace of God. Christ has been relegated to the shadow of
some human personality or a revelation subsequent to the Bible
has been introduced as divine truth even though it conflicts
with the biblical revelation.

A few years ago some men were arrested for selling imitation perfume. They concocted a cheap substitute for the expensive perfumes, put it in fancy bottles with famous labels, and
sold it for the real thing. We must not be deceived by labels
or pious pretensions. The substance in the bottle is what matters. Unless the gospel presented is true to the biblical image
of Christ, it is a fraud.

Only that faith rooted in Christ as the Son of God, our
crucified and risen Savior, will enable our hearts to flourish
with real joy and our souls to prosper with eternal life.

# 4

## The Best Dressed Christian

COLOSSIANS 3:1–14

Wernher Von Braun, the famous missile expert, was the principal speaker for a special occasion at William Jewell College in which I was also participating. The president of the college gave me a unique insight into Dr. Von Braun when he told me that the scientist had requested that his honorarium should be sent to the little church back in Oak Ridge, Tennessee, which he attended. This was evidence that Dr. Von Braun had an appreciation for the spiritual values of life. He was sensitive to the importance of inner space as well as outer space. In these verses, Paul called upon all Christians to be spiritual astronauts. "Seek those things which are above," he instructed.

### With Your Head in the Clouds

We are to live, so to speak, with our head in the clouds. Ordinarily, we think of a person with his head in the clouds as one who is very impractical and unrealistic. As a Christian, the focus of our lives, however, is to be on things above and not on things on earth. This is a very difficult instruction for us earthlings. We are born of the dust of the earth, and we have a very real affinity for earthly things. We experience the fleshly cravings and appetites of earth beings. Somebody has said, "Heaven calls but earth clings." Survival here on this earthly sphere becomes a matter of urgency. We sometimes call it "making a living." We lie awake at night worrying about how we are going to pay our debts.

Life is not easy in this twentieth century because so many luxuries have become necessities. Survival is not just bread on the table but two cars in the garage and perhaps a membership in the country club. Beyond survival, there is the need to exist as comfortably as possible. Comfort takes on more sophisticated interpretations every day. Comfort means air-conditioned homes, king-size beds, color TV, and wall-to-wall carpeting. Comfort means extensive and expensive vacations, steak dinners with candlelight and soft music, children at prestige colleges. There are times in the midst of this good life of the twentieth century when we envy the simple existence of our ancestors who had nothing to cope with but Comanches, outlaws, drought, and boll weevils.

How can we live with our head in the clouds when Uncle Sam keeps our nose to the grindstone in order that we can pay our taxes? The high cost of living keeps our spirits low. We visit the grocery store and break out in a cold sweat at the increase of prices. Our whole pattern of life is designed to keep us earthbound. Our spirit simply can't soar when we are so burdened down with earthly and material concerns.

Furthermore, man has his own contrary nature to cope with. Really, I doubt if it has ever been easy to escape the clutches of materialism and mundane interests. Think of Adam and Eve who in the cool of the evening walked in the Garden with God. Surely, they had no problem setting their affection on things above. But there was a snake in the grass that turned their attention earthward and inward. Our primitive parents became absorbed in their own selfish interests and began to think more about what they were going to put in their stomachs and on their backs than of God.

There is a snake in the grass today, also, which entices us to become fascinated with the things of this world. How dull at times religion seems in comparison to cars, clothes, sex, money, sports, and dozens of other things that dominate our thoughts and affections. We must face the fact that we are of this world—worldly. It does not come naturally to us to set our affections on things above. We may glance in that direction occasionally, but our real interests lie here on this earthly plane. There is something coarse, vulgar, and earthy in the makeup of everyone of us. It becomes exceedingly difficult to rise above this crass nature. How can we seek things above when we can't get our feet out of the mud?

## A New Person

There isn't much chance that we can live with our head in the clouds unless something very drastic happens to liberate us from the gravitational pull of this earth. Paul said it is something as drastic as death, burial, and resurrection. In becoming a Christian, we go through a spiritual experience in which we die to the old self and are raised a new person in Christ. That old nature, so crass and craven, is deposited like a corpse in the obscurity of our past; through the Christ, we emerge a new and better self, capable of living by the ideals of heaven. The realization of this potential is not accomplished without spiritual discipline, even in the life of a Christian. The very words Paul used imply an energetic effort upon our part for we are to *"seek* things above," and to *"set* our affections on things above." This does not mean spending our days in a perpetual prayer meeting. It does involve a conscious commitment of self to Jesus Christ day by day.

Years ago, E. Stanley Jones, a missionary to India, met Mahatma Gandhi and asked him, "What must Christians do to win India for the Lord Jesus Christ?" Gandhi's reply sets forth some of the principles by which the new person in Christ must live if he is a real spiritual astronaut. Gandhi said that, first of all, Christians must live like Jesus Christ. Secondly, they must not compromise their faith. Thirdly, they must learn all they can about the non-Christian religions, and fourthly, they must let everything they do be characterized by love. The apostle Paul would probably have agreed with Gandhi in his characterization of effective Christian living.

Paul hastened to add a word of warning as well as expectancy. The expectancy is the thrilling anticipation of the returning of Jesus Christ in glory. The implied warning, I believe, is that we will not expect to be completely like Jesus in this life. The full realization of our glory as Christians awaits that glad day of Christ's coming when we shall be with him and like him. In the meantime, Paul offered some very definite instructions about things we can and must do as Christians if we are to live consistently with the miracle of our risen self.

When Thomas Jefferson was president, he customarily took an early morning horseback ride around Washington. One day, he was stopped by a Connecticut Yankee and asked if he was interested in a horse trade. The man did not realize that it was the president whom he was addressing. When the president indicated he was not interested in selling his horse, the conversation turned to politics.

The man freely expressed his dislike for the president, saying that he had heard that the president was a very wasteful man and lived extravagantly. "They tell me," he said, "that he never goes out but he's got clothes on his back that will sell for a plantation. He has rings on his fingers and a frill to his shirt." Jefferson laughingly assured the man that the president usually went out dressed no better than himself. By this time, they were nearing the White House. Jefferson indicated that he knew the president and invited the man to stop by with him and meet the chief executive. When they were in the entrance hall, a servant addressed Jefferson as "Mr. President"; whereupon, the Yankee fled in embarrassment.

## The Garments of the Godless

In what style shall the Christian dress? The new person in Christ must completely dispose of those garments associated with the old way. A new life calls for a new wardrobe. Most of us have some clothing in our closet we wouldn't wear for anything because it is out of style. Fashion changes so fast that it keeps us in a financial frenzy. This year's latest creation quickly becomes last year's old rag. Ties are wider, skirts are longer, pocketbooks thinner, and charge accounts fatter, but who cares, we are in style. We need to be just as style conscious when it comes to Christian ideals. Paul encouraged the Christian to be a moral fashion plate. How unbecoming for a Christian to live as though he dressed out of a rag bag rather than being clothed by God's fashion expert, the Holy Spirit.

On television several years ago, we saw Prince Charles being invested as the Prince of Wales. Wouldn't it have been ridiculous for him to have appeared in a patched suit three times too small and for those who conducted the ceremony to put on his back a dirty, shabby overcoat and an old beaten-up hat on his head? Instead, we saw him cloaked in ermine and a crown placed on his head. This was the true princely style. The Christian is a person who has been invested by the authority and power of God as a prince of his kingdom. It is fitting that the Christian should dress in the style of heaven's royalty.

R. G. Lee tells the story of a woman who came to see him early one morning at his study. She was gaudily dressed and highly rouged. Her bizarre attire was crowned with a tremendous, artificial, white fur piece around her neck. The woman told Lee that the previous evening she had stood outside the church and heard him preach. He had said that Christ would accept a surrendered desert. "My life is a desert," she declared. "Will Christ accept me?" Whereupon, Lee assured her of Christ's loving concern and led her to accept him as her Savior. She left Lee's study by the back door and went directly to a garbage can. She lifted the lid and dropped the white fur piece in the can and slammed down the lid. There are some things, said Paul, that we ought to deposit in the spiritual garbage can as being unworthy of a Christian.

First of all, he said, "Put off anger and wrath." These words are similar, but as Paul used them, they have a different significance. Anger is a general disposition; whereas, wrath is a sudden flare-up of temper. There are people who go around in a mad all the time. They are out of sorts with the world and everything in it. It is as though their minds were soaked in gasoline so that any little spark will set them off. They have a nitroglycerine temper that will blow up at the slightest jar. Some of the quietest, calmest people can be like a seething volcano on the inside. Christ will put out that fire if we will let him.

When Eisenhower was ten years of age, his mother gave

permission to his two older brothers to go trick or treating on Halloween. She told Ike he was too young to go along. He argued and pled but to no avail. He was so completely beside himself that he went up to an old apple tree trunk in the backyard and began pounding on it with all his might until his fists were bleeding. His father grabbed him by the shoulders and sent him to bed. About an hour later, his mother came into the room where Ike was still sobbing into his pillow. The mother sat in a rocking chair beside the bed and said nothing for a long time. Then she began to talk to Ike about temper and controlling it. Eventually, she said, "He that conquers his own soul is greater than he that taketh a city." All the while, she was putting salve on his injured hands and bandaging them. Ike said, "I have always looked back on that conversation as one of the most valuable in my life."

Malice is another garment for the garbage can. This is a spiteful attitude toward others, a cold, calculated desire to see them hurt. Instead of wishing the best for them, you get a satisfaction out of their misfortune. Malice is a cultivated ill will that harbors grudges and nurses hates. Woodrow Wilson was one of the finest Christians ever to sit in the White House, but according to his biographers, he had a problem with this matter of feeling ill will toward those who opposed him. Senator Henry Cabot Lodge and Wilson became bitter political foes. Both were professing Christians, but their personal rancor detracted from their Christian image.

The son-in-law of Woodrow Wilson was the dean of Washington Cathedral. Henry Cabot Lodge's daughter-in-law attended the Cathedral and became a good friend with the dean. Neither of these in-laws shared the animosity of the elders. One day, Mrs. Lodge fell in the church and injured her hip. Dean Sayer helped her across the street to catch a cab. Parked outside of the church was a Rolls Royce in which the widow of Woodrow Wilson was sitting, waiting for her son-in-law. Bessie Lodge limped to the car and said, "Good morning, Mrs. Wilson." Edith Wilson simply turned stonily away, hating all Lodges to the bitter end.

Blasphemy and filthy communication are unbecoming garments for the born-again Christian. Abusive, ugly, foulmouthed language seemingly is becoming more common. There was a time when taking the name of God in vain was a legal offense. In Maryland, back in the colonial days, a decree was passed that anyone heard blaspheming the name of God would have his tongue bored through. A second offense would be punished by having a large letter "B" burned on their head for "Blasphemer." A third offense would be punished by death without benefit of clergy. Our ears are no longer tender to such words. We hear them on the stage, screen, and television. The four-letter word is invading our so-called polite conversations. This language of the gutter no matter how acceptable will never be in style for the Christian.

Lying is also an ugly, unfashionable garment for the Christian. Babe Didrickson Zaharias, the famous woman athlete, hit her golf ball into the rough during a tournament. Upon finding what she thought was her ball, she drove it to the green and putted it into the cup. When she took the ball from the cup, much to her horror, she realized that it was not her ball at all. Technically, this disqualified her from the tournament. However, no one else knew what she had done. How easy it would have been for her to keep silent. Instead, she called attention to what she had done and was disqualified rather than lie. This is the kind of personal integrity that should be characteristic of the Christian.

## The Stylish Christian

The duchess of Windsor, for whom the king of England surrendered his throne, often made the list of the ten best-dressed women in the world. Elsa Maxwell, Washington socialite, once asked the duchess why she devoted so much time and attention to such frivolous things as clothes. She replied that her husband had given up everything for her. "If everyone looks at me when I enter a room, my husband can feel proud of me. That's my chief responsibility." Our Lord Jesus Christ gave up everything for us. Our greatest ambition in life should be to so live that he can be proud of us.

Paul now approached the subject positively and mentioned some virtues in which every Christian is to clothe himself if he is to be well dressed. These are all characteristics that are in keeping with the life-style of the new man in Christ. Paul spoke of Christians as the "elect of God, holy and beloved." These were words that were used of the Jews in the Old Testament. Paul was saying that Christians are now the special people of God and should behave themselves accordingly.

"Bowels of mercies," or compassion, is a very distinctive garment of the well-dressed Christian. The church has been defined as "the company of the concerned." Dr. Christian Bernard, the first man to transplant the human heart, once said, "It is immoral to bury a usable heart." Christ has given the Christian a new heart, and it is, indeed, immoral for him to bury that heart. He should keep it beating with love for all people. John Glenn, the astronaut, once fell in his bathtub and injured himself so severely that he was disqualified from further space exploits. The fall disturbed his equilibrium. When something happens to our love, we lose our spiritual equilibrium. Rather than living with our head in the clouds, we are more apt to fall on our faces.

Kindness, humbleness of mind, and meekness, or gentleness, are vital to the wardrobe of a Christian who is going to be in style. When Stephen Foster died, there was found a scrap of paper on which he had written some words that were apparently to be part of a new song he was going to write. The words were, "Dear Hearts and Gentle People." It seems to me that these words form an appropriate definition of the true Christian attitude.

Long-suffering, forbearance, and forgiveness also rest with great appropriateness upon the Christian. These are in the spirit of Christ, who also forgave us. Perhaps there are no Christian accessories more difficult to wear with sincerity than these three. Sometimes we theoretically forgive others, but down in our hearts we are seething with rage and intolerance. Ian MacClaren said, "Always be kind, for everyone you meet is fighting a hard battle." These words are so true. A little bit of understanding goes a long way toward making life more pleasant for us, as well as for people we encounter.

"Above all these things," said Paul, "put on love." This is the final touch to the Christian wardrobe. If you have love, then in all likelihood you will have all of the other garments that go with it. Love blends them into a harmonious scheme.

I was attending a banquet the other night which was supposed to be semiformal. All of the ladies came in long, beautiful evening dresses, but then a couple showed up who somehow had failed to get the word. The man had on a sport shirt and the woman, a street-length dress. They felt awkward and embarrassed and started to leave. It was only at the encouragement of their friends that they remained for the banquet. It is a good feeling to be appropriately dressed for any occasion. There is a certain ease and grace about the person who is outfitted in the latest styles. In a spiritual sense, the apostle Paul identified this feeling as peace. The more completely we are able to dress in the Christian habiliments, the more perfectly we feel at peace with ourselves and with our God.

One year in college I roomed with another preacher boy. We were both having a very difficult time financially getting through school. One day, he received word from a clothing store in a nearby city to come and pick up a suit that someone had purchased for him. I accompanied him to the store. He was taken to a rack of fine suits and told to pick out whatever he desired. This was a welcomed addition to his meager wardrobe, and he felt very grateful to his unknown benefactor. Christ wants to dress us in heaven's best. He will take the ugliness and sin out of our lives and cloak us in his forgiveness and grace. All of the Christian garments Paul talked about are already paid for through the generosity of Christ, and we have only to go to the trouble of claiming them and adorning ourselves with them.

# 5

## Makes You Love Everybody

COLOSSIANS 3:15 to 4:1

A minister was emphasizing in his sermon the importance of love as a primary Christian characteristic. He asked the question, "How many of you love everybody?" An old codger stood up and said, "Preacher, there ain't nobody I hate. All them critters that done me wrong are already dead." Sometimes it is more of a problem to love the living than the dead. We can sentimentalize about the dead, but the living have uncanny ways of irritating and exasperating us. These live encounters put our Christianity to a real test. I was very disturbed about the acrimonious attitude of one of my parishioners toward a couple of other men in the community. I asked him, "If they came to you and asked your forgiveness, you would forgive them, wouldn't you?"

The bitter reply came back, "No, I would not forgive them."

An unloving and unforgiving spirit is completely contrary to the example and teachings of Jesus. Such an attitude will contaminate our other Christian virtues. It's like pouring sour cream on a bowl of cereal.

Pearl S. Buck, the famous author, at the age of eighty wrote an article for the *Family Weekly* entitled, "What I Now Believe." She confessed that because of her education by a Confucian scholar when she was growing up in China, she used to believe that people were born good and were naturally loving. Across the decades of her life she had changed her mind. She now believes that whether a person is born good or evil depends largely upon the genes which he helplessly inherits. She feels that love is a very transient experience, even in a family. Children love their parents only as long as the parents are necessary. Human beings are not naturally loving, she declares. Love is an attribute that must be cultivated.

The Bible teaches that we human beings enter this world with an inclination toward evil rather than good. The validation of this is rather easily demonstrated when we ask ourselves the question, Is it easier to be good or to be bad? We can drift into evil, but we have to strive to be good. We are essentially, therefore, selfish, self-loving, self-protective individuals. In the new birth, a significant change takes place. To be good and to love everybody becomes a more natural disposition. The person in Christ participates in Christ's loving nature. The line of demarcation between the sinner and the Christian is never more clearly indicated than in this matter of attitude toward others. Jesus said, "By this shall all men know that ye are my disciples, if ye have love one to another" (John 13:35).

## Armistice Day

When I was a youngster, the celebration of Armistice Day on November 11 was always an important occasion in our community. I was once asked to read the poem "In Flander's Field" to the people assembled in the cemetery for a program honoring those who had given their lives in World War I. We remembered the price they had paid for the peace we enjoyed. Paul reflected back to Calvary where the price of our peace was paid by the Prince of Peace. When the love of Christ becomes our prevailing disposition, peace is its most natural by-product. We have peace with God and with our fellowman.

Captain Eddie Rickenbacker, the World War I flying ace, tells us in his autobiography that he was flying over no-man's-land at eleven o'clock on Armistice Day. He was the only audience for one of the greatest shows ever presented. When the word passed along the trenches that the war was over, brown-uniformed men poured out of the American trenches and gray-green-uniformed men poured out of the German. Rickenbacker watched from his lofty vantage point as men threw their helmets in the air, discarded their guns, and waved their hands. All up and down the front, the two groups of men began edging toward each other. A few moments before, they had been trying to shoot each other, but now suddenly gray uniforms mixed with brown. He could see the men hugging each other, dancing and jumping. He flew up to the French sector and saw something even more incredible. After four years of trying to slaughter each other, the French and the Germans were not only hugging but also kissing each other on both cheeks.

Armistice day occurs for the Christian the moment he accepts Christ as Savior. Ideally, he is at peace with the whole world. He lays aside his hostilities and animosities and opens his arms in a brotherly embrace to all humanity. Practically, we all know we have to grow in this grace of loving others. Peace is the immediate impulse of the Christian experience, but personal discipline is required to put it into practice.

Cameron Townsend, a pioneer in the literacy ministry, went with his wife to a little town outside of Mexico City. They lived there for awhile in order to learn the language and to share the gospel. Don Martin was the mayor of the community. He and Townsend soon became fast friends. The mayor had many enemies, however, and carried a pistol. One day, he asked to borrow the little book from which the missionary had been reading to him and began sharing it with the hangers-on at the municipal building.

After some time, Martin came to Townsend and said, "Something has happened to me. I can't lie or get drunk as I used to. I have quit beating my woman. This book stops me." He purchased some of the New Testaments, saying that he was going to send one to each of his chief enemies, along with a letter declaring that this book had helped him to forgive them and expressing the hope that they would also read it and forgive him. He explained to the missionary that he had also put away his gun. Whereupon, Townsend exclaimed, "Don Martin, you have been spiritually reborn."

If human intellect, culture, and scientific advance could produce peace, then surely the twentieth century would have been the most peaceful in the existence of man. Instead, it has been a century of violence, a century of the kaiser, Hitler, Stalin, Tojo, Hiroshima, Auschwitz, and napalm. Peace cannot be achieved, however. It has to be received. The kind of peace the world gives is like a beautifully wrapped Christmas box with nothing on the inside. It has no substance or permanency because it is based upon nothing more substantial than wishful thinking. The peace of Christ, on the other hand, is the bountiful overflow of the divinely inspired spirit of love in the heart of the Christian.

## The Grace of Gratitude

If there were any admonition in the Scriptures that should be superfluous, it would be the words of Paul, "Be ye thankful." Gratitude should be the most immediate and spontaneous reaction in our hearts to God's love and blessings. I was so happy and thankful when I became a Christian, I could hardly contain myself. There is a difference, however, between this immediate effervescent, spontaneous feeling of thankfulness and the abiding characteristic of gratitude.

Gratitude is a prevailing disposition and not a momentary feeling of exhilaration. Gratitude is a distinctive Christian grace. Paul, in characterizing the ungodly, wicked people in his letter to the Romans, said, "They are not thankful" (Rom. 1:21, author's paraphrase). Ungodly people live in God's world, enjoying God's bounty without ever giving God so much as a thank you. Time after time in Paul's writings, he paused to praise and thank God. "Thanks be unto God for his unspeakable gift" (2 Cor. 9:15). "But thanks be to God, which giveth us the victory through our Lord Jesus Christ" (1 Cor. 15:57). "Now thanks be unto God, which giveth us the victory through our Lord Jesus Christ" (2 Cor. 2:14). There is a spontaneity and genuineness in these expressions which should also characterize our spirit.

Gratitude should be the predominate note in all of our worship experiences. When the church family gets together, it is for the purpose of celebrating the victory in Christ and expressing gratitude to God for his grace. Gratitude that is not expressed will soon dissipate. This is one of the reasons that Christian worship is so urgently needed by every child of God. If we do not praise God for his blessings, we begin taking them for granted.

The communal experience of praising God together with other Christians is mutually stimulating. It helps strengthen the love bond between Christians as we join in songs of thanksgiving. It helps create a family feeling in the church. The people of God are congealed into a mighty force for good by the common experience of gratitude. Thanksgiving is a powerful motivation for Christian service. A woman who was happily converted in her latter years, feeling that she was ungifted for some of the more glamorous jobs in the church, said to me when she came forward at the service, "I want to do the things nobody else will do." Gratitude will inspire people to tithe, to witness, to attempt things for God which would seem impossible under other circumstances.

The summer after my first year in college, I was preaching in small country churches in my county. I had only two or three sermons, which presented no problem because I preached in a different church each Sunday. When one church invited me back the next Sunday, I was in trouble. For some reason, I had not found time to prepare a sermon for Sunday evening. After lunch I went out into the woods where I could be alone and think. A sermon just would not come. It was getting closer to the time to go to the church. I finally settled on a text and two or three general ideas. I prayed, "Lord, you got me into this, and now you're going to have to get me out."

A very strange thing happened that night. The Lord gave me great liberty, and the service seemed to be charged with his presence. When I gave the invitation, people started coming forward. I had never had a profession of faith in one of my services before this. That night, six adults accepted Christ. It was a time of great thanksgiving in my heart, as though Christ were saying to me, "I've called you and I will enable you." The lesson I learned was not that I should never prepare sermons but that prepared or not, the victory comes through Christ and not through my feeble efforts. Gratitude beyond anything else will cause us to attempt things for Christ that we cannot do alone.

## With Naught Save Love

For years, at almost every wedding I performed, it seemed someone sang, "Because you come to me with naught save love." This is love's idealism at its rosiest. With what blissful ignorance most of us entered into marriage! The youth of today are just as unrealistic. When they stand at the marriage altar, they still feel that love is enough. Although they have not usually thought about it, they are bringing into their marriage a great deal more than just love. They bring themselves, for example, with their backgrounds, personalities, egos, psychological hang-ups, likes, and dislikes, and a whole lot of other things that will vitally influence their relationship. While love is basic to their happiness, there are other factors which can bang that love around until it stands helplessly by while the home disintegrates. The astonishing divorce rate is evidence enough that love alone will not make a marriage work.

Dr. John Sutherland Bonnell, one of the most successful pastor-counselors of this century, has written that in three decades of counseling, he never encountered an experience of marital failure in a home where religion was a vital factor. One of the secrets of success in marriage is not only marrying the right person but also in being the right person. Most family problems arise because of our own irascibility, selfishness, pride, and just plain meanness. Having Christ in our lives takes a great deal of the abrasiveness out of our personalities and helps us to establish happy, interpersonal relationships. This is particularly important in the home where we live in such intimacy with other members of the family.

Dear Abby received a letter from a mother of four who had wanted a divorce but patiently hung on. She said that she was glad she did because her husband's life had been changed after he accepted Christ while watching Billy Graham on television. Accepting Christ won't settle all family problems, but it does provide a base upon which a happy marriage can be built. Wayne Dehoney has written a book called *Homemade Happiness.* Our homes are still what we make them, and Christ is our most effective ally in creating a happy home.

Paul offered some practical counsel for Christian families, and he began with the wives. "Wives, submit yourselves unto your own husbands, as it is fit in the Lord" (v. 18). The women may say, "Well, that sounds just like a man," or the henpecked husband may remind us that Paul was an armchair strategist where marriage was concerned because, evidently, he remained a bachelor. It is clear from the context that by submissiveness Paul did not mean obsequiousness. He did not assign the wife to a role of being a fawning nobody. In a successful marriage, there has to be some give-and-take. In the Christian home, the husband is viewed as the leader. In the larger biblical context, the wife is the helpmate. She submits in the sense that her goals, lifework, ambition, and energies must be blended with those of her husband. This does not mean that she forfeits her self-worth, dignity, or even her happiness. She will find her greatest fulfillment, however, in being supportive to her husband and in forming with him a creative and enduring bond.

The Christian husband will have the utmost respect and affection for his wife and treat her with all the courtesy and dignity becoming to one who has devoted herself to him. It is Christ who will help husbands and wives overcome the pride and selfishness which makes such a relationship impossible. In my own counseling, I find that usually a rededication to Jesus Christ will go a long way toward solving all the other problems in the home. When people's hearts are right with God, they can get right with each other.

The American Institute of Family Relations compared one hundred unhappy marriages, which had been referred to them, to one hundred happy marriages. They made the discovery that the greatest single difference in the two was the extent to which affection was demonstrated. They said that husbands sometimes are victims of the taboo of tenderness and their wives become emotionally starved.

Another study has revealed that young people who make the most successful marriages are those whose parents not only loved each other but also were quite demonstrative in showing their love in the presence of the children. Many women can sympathize with the Nashville housewife who during the football season put an ad in the newspaper which read, "For Sale: Husband and TV set, cheap."

Paul continued with a word of advice for children, saying that obedience to parents is a basic way for them to show their love for Jesus. This assumes, of course, that the parents are the kind of people that children can honor. Everything Paul said was predicated upon a genuine Christian identity in the home. A pastor took a group of underprivileged children from the city on a camp-out. As they walked along a trail, one of the boys said to him, "Mister, what is God like?" The pastor, seeking to make his explanation as simple as possible, replied, "Well, Son, God is like a father."

The boy immediately responded, "Well, if God is like my father, I sure would hate him."

The very fact that God is called Father indicates that human fathers are to present their children with the image of love, tenderness, and care. One of the distressing features of family life brought to light today is the abuse of children. There are other ways of abusing children, however, than by physically beating them. It is the very unfortunate child who is denied the example of a Christian father and mother.

A national magazine carried an article sometime ago entitled, "Lead Poisoned Kids." It said that about two hundred children die each year from lead poisoning. Many more are treated and survive but half of them are left mentally retarded. Where do they get this lead poisoning? Lead paint has not been used on the interiors of buildings for a number of years, but in old buildings it lies just beneath the surface of newer coats of lead-free paint. When the walls are not properly maintained, the old paint lifts away in layered chips along with the new. This is particularly a condition in slum housing. There are some children who seem to have a craving for nonfood substances, and they eat these flakes of paint. The result is lead poisoning.

Children are either spiritually blessed or cursed by the kind of home in which they have been reared. Many of them reach adulthood with their minds poisoned against religion because of the insincerity, the inconsistency, and the hypocrisy of parents who presumably are Christians. One of the most difficult persons to reach for Christ is that adult who had an unfortunate experience with Christianity in the home as a child. It has spread cynicism and doubt and left him with a hurt which makes him exceedingly leery where Christ and the church are concerned. President Eisenhower was frequently asked why there had not been any black sheep in his family. He explained it by saying that his family was free from parental quarreling and filled with genuine love. The fact that his father and mother were devout Christians, no doubt, contributed to this atmosphere of congeniality.

## Christianity on the Job

The terms "slave" and "master" could be translated into modern terminology as *labor* and *management*. Can, indeed, Christianity be expressed on the job? Paul felt that it was Christian for the workman to be diligent, resourceful, productive, and able to take instruction to the point that Christ would be proud of him. Christian management does not seek to exploit but rather to be equitable and fair in their dealings with labor. This would seem to be a bit naive in today's world.

Mary C. Crowley was determined to put Christian principles into operation in the business world. She was relieved of one job because of these ideals. Whereupon, she founded her own company. She sells decorative items for the home and has a work force of thousands of women. She has sought to inculcate in her sales people the principle of Christian love and genuine concern for the customer. Her company seems to be one big family. She is exceedingly generous with her employees, and her business has grown dramatically. She conceives of her business enterprise as a service to God and fellowman. She has put her philosophy and her experiences in a recent book called *Think Mink*. On the surface, it may appear sanctified materialism, but, in reality, she is a living demonstration that Christianity can be expressed in the business world.

Love is, indeed, a many splendored thing. Christ in our lives, however, will make love even more splendid because its focus will not be upon a selective few. It makes you love everybody.

# 6

## A Warm Hand in the Dark

COLOSSIANS 4:2–9,12–13,15–18

When Helen Keller was a little girl, her parents took her to the home of Alexander Graham Bell, the inventor of the telephone. Bell was greatly moved by the plight of this child who could neither see nor hear. He took her in his arms and she felt the tenderness of his concern. It was partly by the methods introduced by Bell that Helen was taught to communicate. One day, she wrote a letter to the inventor in which she said, "Dear Mr. Bell, I do love you." More than thirty years later when Bell was seventy-one, Helen again wrote him, "Even before my teacher came, you held out a warm hand to me in the dark."

Paul's letter to the Colossians was like a warm hand reaching out to them in Christian love. His words communicated genuine concern and gave them heart to press on living for Jesus in a difficult day. Christian fellowship serves this purpose in our time. Christians should always be alert to their opportunities to reach out a warm hand of encouragement both to their fellow Christians and those outside the fold. Paul mentioned some of the ways of doing this in chapter 4.

### Thankful Prayer

Paul asked for the prayers of the Colossian Christians. How else could they reach him in that faraway prison cell? Prayer is often the only and the best way to help others. It is interesting that Paul asked that the Colossians' prayers be characterized by thanksgiving. Thankfulness is the essence of genuine prayer. Too often, our prayers are petitions and complaints rather than praise. Most of us could pick a quarrel with God if we were so inclined. We could lay at his feet a long list of burdens, heartaches, and seeming injustices. How unfair it is to go through life grumbling, however, when God has given us so many things for which to be grateful.

I have reached that time in life where I have to wear bifocals. The upper part of the lens enables me to see at a distance with greater clarity. The lower part of the lens enables me to see things near at hand. If I try to look at distant objects through the lower half, I simply see a blur. Sometimes, we are inclined to focus on our troubles because they are so close to us, but the overview of life is just a blur.

Every day should be thanksgiving day for people as blessed as we are. We live in an Aladdin's world where people go to the moon, and we can watch them on television. This is the age of wonder drugs and of conveniences completely unknown to previous generations. Our danger is that we take for granted all of these blessings rather than being grateful. Gratitude is an important Christian trait to cultivate. It opens the door to many other fine attributes. Cicero once said, "A thankful heart is not only the greatest virtue but the parent of all other virtues." You never knew an ungrateful person who was also kind and loving and generous. All of the other Christian graces seem to hinge upon this one of thankfulness. It is important, then, from time to time to stop and count our blessings. Among the very first is the privilege of being alive. Sometimes we don't appreciate our years until they have almost run out. Oliver Wendell Holmes, the great jurist, when approaching the age of ninety said to Dean Acheson, "If that ceiling should open and through the opening should come the voice of God saying, 'Wendell, you have five minutes to live,' I should reply, 'Very well, Boss, but I wish it were ten.' "

I am very thankful for people who have enlarged my world. The world in which I grew up was a little secluded town in the Ozark Hills. I was landlocked but not mindlocked. Very early, there were people who began to give me visions of places beyond. Among them were my teachers. Teachers have given many people visions of places beyond. A housewife was cleaning out her attic and came across an old geography book. As she leafed through its dusty pages, she remembered the spinster teacher who made her aware of faraway places. She sat down and wrote a note to the teacher thanking her for doing more than teaching geography. A short time later, she received a reply from the teacher, a letter written in the telltale scrawl of age. She said, "You are the first person of all my years of teaching who ever said thank you."

How often do we take time to thank God who gave us this wonderful world and the privilege of living in it? We should thank him, also, for the people who serve our needs everywhere we go, people who put the food on our tables, the clothes on our backs, the gas in our tanks, produce the electricity which lights our homes, and the hands that heal our bodies. We take millions of people for granted who perform tasks necessary for our comfort. This thought reminds me of a story concerning the Pilgrim fathers' treatment of an Indian who had tried to help them. In preparation for the first Thanksgiving, the Indian had hastened to the forest, eager to supply his bit to the white man's feast. He killed a deer and carried it to the settlement, proudly presenting it to his new friends. Rather than expressing appreciation, they had him whipped because he had killed the deer on Sunday. I wonder what he thought of his new Christian friends? Our lack of gratitude is also a cruel lash to those who serve us.

The supreme reason for our thankful prayers is the grace of God. What if God were vindictive and bent upon judgment alone? His very existence would be a curse to us. Instead, he is a God of love and mercy. He loves us in spite of who we are and is intent upon blessing us. John said, "We love him, because he first loved us" (1 John 4:19).

A seven-year-old girl was busy with crayons and scissors and paste and cardboard. Presently, she came to the kitchen where her mother was working and said, "Mother, you do so many nice things for us, I've made a badge for you." The mother permitted the daughter to pin the badge on her and across it were scrawled the words, "I love you." Every prayer should pin a badge on God in which we express our loving appreciation for his attendant mercies. Only then have we properly set the stage to offer our petitions.

## A Wise Walk

Paul used an expression in verse 5 that sends cold chills up my spine. He identifies non-Christians as "them that are without." In other words, the outsiders. Several images come to my mind. The first image is that of being in the comfort of my home on a cold, rainy day. Looking out the window, I see some soul struggling along the street, his raincoat pulled up tight around him, and think, "I'm glad that's not me out there." Another image is that of a soldier who has scrambled into the safety of a bunker and looks out to see his buddies falling under the withering fire of the enemy. What a difference it makes to be on the inside.

To the person on the inside, a wall represents security. The inspired writer in the book of Revelation described heaven as "a walled city," the wall rising 216 feet. This is the symbolism of complete security. Nothing can breach the wall of heaven to destroy us. Isaiah described the new Jerusalem by saying, "thou shalt call thy walls Salvation" (Isa. 60:18). The Christian is the one who is within the walls of salvation. We are like sheep safely in the fold. Paul spoke of non-Christians as being "without Christ, . . . having no hope, and without God in the world (Eph. 2:12). I stood one cold, rainy day on a platform and gazed over the cruel wall that runs through the heart of Berlin. I found myself thinking about those people on the other side who have no freedom, living in fear and intimidation. I made a brief excursion beyond that wall, but I had no desire to stay. I felt much more comfortable when, at last, I was on this side again.

People without Christ are tyrannized by their sin and are living under the judgment of death. I have made brief excursions into that world when I have been asked to preach the funeral of a person who was not a Christian or whose family was without Christ. It is a forlorn existence and I want no part of it. This does not mean that I should look from the security of my position with smugness, censoriousness, or indifference upon those without. We are to love them and to do all that we can to attract them to the inside by encouraging them to put their trust in Christ as Savior.

Paul said, "Walk in wisdom toward them that are without" (v. 5). He meant that our daily conduct in the presence of non-Christians should exemplify the Christian ideals. We are walking advertisements. By our behavior, we convince people on the outside that we have discovered something exceedingly worthwhile. Outsiders are often very skeptical about the Christian claims, and they have a right to see a living demonstration.

Bet-A-Million Gates was a fabulous character of the last century. He came to Texas with a franchise to sell barbed wire to the ranchers. He had a difficult job convincing the ranchers that his thin strands would contain their wild steers. Whereupon, Gates made a corral with his barbed wire on one of the plazas in San Antonio. He invited the ranchers to bring their wildest steers and put them in the corral. It was a gala occasion as the ranchers came from far and wide on the appointed day. At a signal, the steers were stampeded into the barbed wire. They hit the wire, bounced off, and stood back looking somewhat dumbfounded but did not try it again. The ranchers were convinced, and Bet-A-Million Gates could not fill all the orders for his barbed wire. Outsiders are waiting to be convinced of the genuineness of Christianity through the difference that Christ has made in our daily conduct.

I like Weymouth's translation of the words, "redeeming the time." He puts it like this: "Seizing your opportunities." Paul was concerned about our seizing our opportunities to witness for Christ to those who are on the outside. This implies an aggressive spirit. One translator has put it like this: "Buy up your opportunities." Buy them up like a housewife snapping up bargains when she sees them. It is usually the case that if you don't buy the bargain at the moment, when you go back it is gone. This is also true quite often in Christian witness. We should condition ourselves to act instinctively and spontaneously when the opportunity presents itself.

## Graceful Speech

A close relationship with Christ will affect the quality of our speech. Paul said speech will be "seasoned with salt." Salt is what makes food tasty and palatable. The salt in the Christian's language is grace, and through our speech we will reveal a warm and loving heart. It is not the harsh, hard, judgmental voice that reaches souls for Christ.

Eddie Rickenbacker, one of America's most famous fliers, floated around in the South Pacific for many days on a life raft with some other companions after their plane went down. He had a very deep religious experience during those days which became evident in his life afterward. One person put it like this: "Rickenbacker has become an evangelist without knowing it. There is an unworldly gleam in his eyes and a quaver in his voice these days."

Rickenbacker replied, "He was wrong in only one respect. I knew. From the time of the Pacific ordeal, my faith in God was an active, open part of my life."

Maude Adams was one of the most illustrious actresses of the first part of this century. A critic once went to see her performance of Shakespeare's *Merchant of Venice*. He had gone somewhat reluctantly saying, "I went feeling like a hangman. I came out feeling like a messenger bearing a pardon." Those words can be utilized to describe very beautifully the mission of a Christian, "a messenger bearing a pardon." We bear a pardon from God for those on the outside, those who are lost and doomed and without God. Our words should be mellowed by the concern of our hearts and impassioned by the love we bear for those on the outside.

## Fervent Labor

I am usually a bit startled when I come to the end of one of Paul's letters and find a list of people. I have been thinking about an institution called the church as I have been reading his letter, but then I am forcefully reminded that the church is made up of real people, people like Tychicus, a faithful minister; Onesimus, a beloved brother; Epaphras, a servant of Christ. The church is people in various stages of Christian maturity, people who have individual weaknesses and strengths, people who in varying degrees of loyalty are trying to live for Christ in a world that is ruthlessly opposed to him. I am glad that in the life of the church there have been strong, stable persons who have been stack poles to the rest of us.

In the early fall, when I was a boy, my father used to buy the wood for the winter. It came in about four-foot lengths and was stacked by our house waiting to be sawed up for use. At each end of the stack, there was a perpendicular pole which supported and held up the stack. If you removed the stack pole, the whole lot would come tumbling down. This is the role which the stalwart heroes of faith have played in the life of the church across the centuries. Their faithfulness, diligence, and courage have helped to shore up the church. I want my life to be a strength to the Christian community and a positive influence upon my fellow Christians.

What a beautiful compliment Paul paid Epaphras when he described him as "always labouring fervently for you in prayers, that ye may stand perfect and complete in all the will of God." (v. 13).

I don't find many in the church today who labor fervently. There are more reluctant laborers than there are fervent. People sometimes perform Christian work as though it were an onerous chore. It has become exceedingly difficult, for example, to get church members to do personal witnessing. Yet, there is nothing more essential if we are to reach the outsiders for Christ.

Henry Cabot Lodge tells of a plane that was forced down on the Greenland ice cap during world War II. The pilot of a search plane located the downed plane and recognized that an immediate rescue was necessary if the lives of the passengers were to be saved. The only place he could possibly land his seaplane was in a slight depression in the ice cap where the ice had melted just enough to form a thin film of water. Even if a successful landing could be made, there was a very slim chance of his being able to take off again. Nevertheless, he went in and kept his plane circling on the surface of the water so that it would not stick in the slush ice which lay immediately below the few inches of water. Each time his plane went past the group of marooned men, he reached out over the side of his plane and pulled one of them into the cabin. Only his extraordinary strength enabled him to perform the feat of pulling into his moving plane men who were so weakened that they could not help themselves. Finally, all of the men were in the plane and by great skill he was able to lift the plane off the water and fly the men back to home base.

Christians must make the ultimate effort to save the last one who is lost in sin. If we are going to bring the outsiders in, it will require more concentrated effort than most of us are expending at the moment. Few Christians can point to anyone whom they positively know they have led to Christ. We must be wary of sitting safely inside the walls of salvation enjoying our security and exhibiting neither concern nor action to bring the outsiders to Christ.

## Remember My Bonds

Paul concluded his letter to the Colossians with a kind of slogan, "Remember my bonds." Paul probably dictated the letter and then signed it. We can almost hear the chains rattle as he took a pen in hand to affix his signature. Paul was not asking for sympathy but was calling for loyalty. This reminds us of the cry that once rang out in Texas, "Remember the Alamo!" Texans were not announcing a funeral but calling men to arms. In the spirit of those who in past ages have suffered, bled, and died for Christ and for a lost world, may we also be willing to serve and to sacrifice that the church may be a militant, conquering force.

I am sure that the three words, "Remember my bonds," burned themselves into the consciences of the Colossian Christians. Whenever they were inclined to complain about the hardships or inconveniences incurred as Christians, these words lighted up in their minds with neon brilliance. Whenever they grew lax in the service of the Lord, these words rang in their ears. These words also leap from the printed page, today, to remind us that serious Christianity involves a willingness to sacrifice. Elton Trueblood, the Christian philosopher and author, in his autobiography confesses that new strength came into his ministry when he realized that he either had to reject Christ and admiring talk or accept him on his own terms. "I saw that he did not ask for admiration; he asked for commitment!"

# 7

## God Creates No Inferior Products
### PHILEMON 7–21

The singing and testimony of Ethel Waters have been regular features of the Billy Graham crusades for several years. Ethel, who achieved fame in the entertainment industry, dedicated her latter years to witnessing for Christ. Billy Graham gave her a testimonial dinner a few years ago. He asked her how she had maintained such a positive outlook on life despite the racial discrimination she had experienced. Ethel replied, "I have lived out of the belief that God creates no inferior products." When it comes to human beings, there are no factory seconds, castoffs, or rejects. Even Christians have a difficult time absorbing this magnificent biblical truth and accepting each other as equals before God. Cultural conditioning is likely to be such a strong formative factor in our attitudes that the gospel truth often penetrates slowly. It is only as Christian love permeates our spirit that we can overcome our hostilities and biases.

Onesimus was just one of sixty million slaves in the Roman empire, but he was precious in the sight of God. He had the exceeding good fortune of encountering the apostle Paul and learning from him that God loves slaves and masters alike. Onesimus had run away from Philemon, his master, but Philemon was also a runaway from the principle of Christian brotherhood. Paul's effort in his letter to Philemon was to bring master and slave together on the common ground of mutual Christian love.

### The Social Freshener

Paul made a tactical approach to the mind and heart of Philemon with a gracious compliment. Philemon loved his fellow Christians, but perhaps it had never occurred to him to love his slaves. He probably took them and their status for granted. He may have felt a proprietary affection for them but, thus far, had not understood that Christian love extends to all people. Now that Onesimus was a Christian, Philemon was directly confronted with a perplexing situation. The question was whether his Christian love could overpower the prejudice and the common social attitudes toward a people of inferior status.

The interpersonal relationships in modern society are certainly less than ideal. While significant strides have been made in recent years in the area of human rights, still there are malodorous and festering sores to which Christians need to give their attention. Paul said that the hearts of the saints had been refreshed by the love of Philemon. Love is the social freshener. Even crusty old Bertrand Russell, the philosopher, admitted that what is called Christian love is the hope of the world.

A number of years ago, I was traveling home by bus after preaching in a revival meeting. About noon, the bus made a luncheon stop at a small-town cafe. Everyone quickly went in and placed an order. As I sat at the counter waiting for my lunch, I saw through the window a black couple who were passengers, standing alone beside the bus. It occurred to me that they probably would not have felt welcome in the cafe. I was upset at the idea so I went out and asked them if I could order anything for them. They replied that they had brought their food with them.

Late that afternoon, at a bus stop, someone behind me asked, "May I buy you a Coke?" It was the black man whom I had sought to befriend. As we stood drinking the Cokes, I remarked, "I hope I did not embarrass you at noon when I asked if I could purchase some food for you."

"Oh no," he replied, "my sister and I have been on a trip to California, and that was the nicest thing that happened to us on the whole journey."

The communication of Christian love and brotherhood is

often a very simple thing, but it does require a sensitivity to the inequities and injustices all about us.

Our attitudes toward other people are often reflective of our background and personal bias. I don't suppose there is anyone completely free of all prejudice. Race is not the only basis of prejudice. Such things as economic circumstance, culture, nationality, religious denomination, and other factors contribute to these interpersonal tensions. We Texans, for example, are accused of looking upon people from other states as less fortunate. The braggadocio of Texans turns off people elsewhere as was indicated by a contest conducted by a commercial firm in the North. First prize was a one-week, all-paid vacation in Texas. Second prize was a *two-week* paid vacation in Texas. State pride is often just a matter of good-natured rivalry. There are, however, deep-down social cancers which challenge the potency of our Christian experience. Does our relation to Christ endue us with the grace sufficient to heal these unworthy attitudes? Certainly, it can be accomplished only as we mature in the love of Jesus Christ. The power is made available through the Holy Spirit as he gives us insight into our unbrotherly inclinations and the inner resolve to love others without horizon.

## For Love's Sake

The relationship between Paul and Philemon was that of teacher and pupil, shepherd and sheep. Philemon was psychologically and spiritually obligated to Paul for having led him to Christ. Paul might have presumed upon that situation and have spoken authoritatively to Philemon. He could have said, "Philemon, you owe it to me to take Onesimus back and treat him like a brother." Paul recognized, however, that love cannot be commanded nor brotherhood administrated. Love is either spontaneous or it is not love. It cannot be contrived but can be focused. He appealed to Philemon to let the love in which he had embraced his fellow Christians reach out to Onesimus as well. Only love could unshackle the mind of Philemon so that he could receive Onesimus as a brother.

I was reared in a county in Missouri where, as far as I

know, there was not a single black resident. In all of my childhood, I had never had any relationship with a black person. I did not know if I was prejudiced. When I went to college as a ministerial student, I was immediately made superintendent of a black mission by the student volunteer group. We held services on Sunday afternoon and Wednesday night in the home of a black family. I hardly knew what to expect of my own emotions when I went for the first service. In the course of the year, I established a very close bond with this family. The first person I won to Christ after I entered the ministry was a little boy from that home. I learned in this very practical way how Christian love can surmount the barriers imposed by culture and environment.

Christian love will help us escape the pitfall of judging people upon a superficial basis. For example, rather than looking down upon the fallen, we will do what the song says, "Lift up the fallen, Tell them of Jesus the mighty to save." Harry Golden for many years published a paper called *The Carolina Israelite.* Early in his life, he had been sent to the penitentiary for five years on a charge of defrauding in the stock market. His book *Only In America* became a best seller. His publisher received an anonymous note advising him that his author was a swindler and ex-con who victimized widows and orphans. Harry Golden thought he was finished but found that, on the whole, people were accepting him for what he was at the present.

When Golden was on a speaking engagement in the North, he learned that the building which housed his newspaper, as well as his own living quarters, had been destroyed by fire. He had lost his mailing list and his valuable correspondence with famous friends such as Sandburg and Einstein. However, when people across the country learned of his plight, they pitched in to help him recoup. Later on, Golden wrote that this experience had enriched his life beyond his wildest dreams. He said that professional newspapermen across the state and the Christian clergy throughout the South extended a hand of fellowship such as rarely comes to a man in a lifetime.

What a difference it would make in our communities, our churches, and even in our families if we would ask the Lord to help us stop nursing our hates and start nourishing our Christian love. Unfortunately, much of the progress in the area of human rights has had to be accomplished by government fiat rather than by Christian love. The fact that we have been forced to acknowledge the dignity of other human beings has not created the most peaceful circumstances. It is not force but affection that forms the basis of harmonious relationships. Paul could not influence the Roman government to outlaw slavery, but he could encourage a fellow Christian to express the love of Christ to another human being. Brotherhood, then, becomes an individual thing in which each of us gives liberty to the Spirit of Christ within us.

## Sharing the Burden

It is obvious that Paul was deeply burdened for both Onesimus and Philemon. Each was a dear brother in Christ. He wanted to rescue Onesimus, now a Christian, from a life of useless wandering. He wanted to rescue Philemon from a spirit of vindictiveness and of pride that would have prevented him from receiving Onesimus as a Christian brother. Paul viewed himself as the catalyst who would bring about reconciliation and mutual acceptance on the part of the master and slave. In the modern world, also, Christians should feel very keenly the burden of alienated humanity. By our example of Christian love, we can help alleviate the oppressive burden of hostility that hangs over the human race like an ominous cloud. A ray of sunshine bursts through that awesome overcast each time we relate one to one in Christian love.

On a cold wintry day, pedestrians were hurrying along Forty-second Street in New York. It was sleeting, and the streets were slippery. People hardly looked at each other as they passed, their coat collars up about their ears. A young man carrying a heavy valise in one hand and a huge suitcase in the other was slipping and sliding on his way to Grand Central Station. Suddenly, a hand reached out and took the valise.

A voice said, "Let me take one, Brother. Bad weather to have to carry things." Years later, Booker T. Washington, the black educator, said, "That was my introduction to Theodore Roosevelt."

As Christians, we must find ways of reaching out a helping hand to share the burden of those who are carrying heavy loads along a slippery way. Life has cast some of our fellowmen in difficult roles. We can help them overcome their handicaps and live useful lives through our loving concern. Many are defeated or depressed or defiant because their way is so difficult. They are given heart by the fact that somebody cares. Included in this group are people of no particular color, creed, or culture. They are to be found in all walks of life. The old song encourages us, "Look all around you, find someone in need; help somebody today." You may have to look no further than your own neighbor whom you begin to treat not as just somebody who lives next door, but as a person who has a need for affection and encouragement.

Somebody has called this a modern ice age in which we are living. It is the age of the unseeing eye and the unfeeling heart, an age in which other people become fellow living things who get in our way at the traffic light or step on our toes at the movies. We must be wary that our own hearts don't turn into icebergs and that we don't become so consumed with our own interests we have no real concern about others. The love of Jesus in our hearts will thaw the human spirit, and palm trees will wave where once polar bears frolicked.

In one of Tolstoy's short stories, a Russian cobbler named Martin dreamed one night that Christ would visit his shop the next day. The shoemaker's dream was so vivid that, in anticipation of the visit of the Savior, he gave his shop a thorough cleansing and then went to work feverishly at his trade so that the Lord might not find him idle. He kept watching for the Master as the day dragged along. No one came, however, except an old man whom Martin befriended, fed, and provided with a warm overcoat. Then there was a poor mother and her baby to whom the cobbler gave food and clothing. An old apple woman and a street urchin quarreled in front of his shop, and he made peace between them.

That night the old shoemaker sat down to read his Bible. He was disappointed that his dream, after all, had been only a dream. Then a voice called his name, and he saw a strange aura of light in the corner behind the stove. Out into the light stepped the old man, the mother and child, the apple woman and the urchin. Each one smiled and asked, "Martin, did you not know me?" and then vanished. Martin turned back to his Bible where his eye fell upon the verse, "Inasmuch as ye have done it unto one of the least of these my brethren, ye have done it unto me" (Matt. 25:40).

## A Beloved Brother

One of the most difficult words to pronounce from a spiritual standpoint is the word *brother.* Too often, we stumble over it and mumble the word *bother.* I wonder if Philemon had any difficulty calling Onesimus brother. Could Philemon now relate to Onesimus as a fellow citizen of the kingdom in which there is neither slave nor free? I feel sure that Philemon had to do a lot of thinking and praying before he could establish the right Christian relationship with Onesimus. Even though we know the Lord Jesus Christ as Savior, still it requires considerable maturity as a Christian to lay aside traditional attitudes, community patterns, and personal hang-ups. We usually don't stop looking down on others until we spend sufficient time looking up toward God.

Many years ago, a little black boy showed up at a Vacation Bible School I was conducting at a rural church where I was pastor. Some of the church members became exceedingly upset and felt threatened by the presence of the child. I had not realized until then how deeply ingrained were some of their racial feelings. While I could not understand why they felt this way, still I could appreciate the dilemma it presented to them as Christians. They did not need my harassment; they needed my prayers. Frequently, people who feel that they are unprejudiced are deeply prejudiced against the prejudiced.

Paul did not blackball Philemon because he owned a slave. He did not call him unchristian and refuse to have anything to do with him. He appealed to him on the basis of his Christian experience and of his Christian love to receive Onesimus as a brother. Unbrotherliness is never a one-way street. I am sure that Onesimus also had to make some changes in his own attitude about Philemon. After all, he had run away from what he conceived to be an intolerable situation. Would he now run the risk of returning and putting himself at the mercy of Philemon?

Unbrotherly attitudes are not the province of any one race or cultural segment in society. The book of Philemon is a call to each of us to reconsider our attitudes about and the way we treat other people. For most of us, it will not be a once in a lifetime decision; it will be a renewed commitment day by day, that with the help of Jesus, we will relate to other people in brotherly love. If we are true to the Spirit of Christ, this must be our attitude regardless of how others treat us.

As a matter of fact, love is the one thing that will remove the motes from our eyes as we look upon our fellowmen and enable us to accept them in the beauty of their divine origin. I once read a story about a blind man who had fallen in love with a woman of homely features. One day, it was discovered that his sight was gradually being restored to his eyes. In those days, when the vision of the man was clarifying, his beloved wife became increasingly anxious. She was well aware of her plainness and was certain that her husband would be greatly disappointed when at last he could look upon her face.

One evening the many friends of the couple gave a party to celebrate the recovery of sight of their neighbor. The former blind man watched as his wife busied herself with the refreshments. He said to a friend sitting with him, "How fortunate I am that, even though I was blind, I selected such a beautiful woman for my wife." His love for her endowed his wife with all the marks of great beauty.

There is a recent surgical development for persons who have had their vision blurred by cataracts. The obstruction is removed and tiny lens is implanted in their eyes which enables them to have perfect vision. Christ will perform the same service for us in a spiritual sense when we submit to his ministry. He will remove the prejudice and hostility which blur our spiritual vision and make it possible for us to view our fellowmen in the clarity of Christian love.

Paul, who wrote these words, could never forget that day when Ananias came to visit him in the house of Judas on the street called Straight and addressed him as "Brother Saul."

# 8

## A Partnership of Love

PHILIPPIANS 1:1–11

Philippians was Paul's love letter to his favorite church. Never once did he use his pen as a lash in this book. Instead, there flowed from his pen expressions of affection and appreciation. This church was probably the most faithful, thoughtful, and spiritual of all the churches he founded. Paul was writing from a prison cell, but the Philippians' love penetrated through the thick prison walls to cheer his heart. The prisoner Paul lifted his face heavenward and thanked God for this partnership of love which he shared with the Philippian Christians. His words are like a verbal bouquet whose fragrance we can still detect as we read his epistle. We are stimulated in this twentieth century to reappraise the importance and the privilege of sharing in that affectionate fellowship called the church.

Paul existed, for that moment, under the shadow of uncertainty. His fate as a prisoner lay in capricious hands. He did not know whether freedom or execution lay before him. Someone has proposed the question, What would you do if you knew you had only five minutes to say all that needed to be said? You would, no doubt, spend those moments expressing your love to your family and intimate friends. Paul wrote from a sense of deep need to communicate while there was time his boundless affection and gratitude for his dear companions in the gospel at Philippi. In this, he has set a worthy example for us today. How often do we pen a note or speak a word of loving appreciation to our Christian friends? We are far too prone, I am sure, to take these associations for granted. All that is required is a tiny bit of energy plus an abundance of thoughtfulness.

Dean Allen Moon, late professor at William Jewell College,

told a class one day that at every Christmastime, he sat down and wrote a letter to a former teacher back in Alabama who had greatly influenced his life. A year or so later on the campus of Southern Baptist Seminary, I was talking with a fellow student who came from Alabama. When she learned that I had attended William Jewell College, she asked, "Oh, did you know Dean Moon? Every year at Christmastime, my grandfather, now in his nineties, receives a letter from Dean Moon thanking him for the encouragement he gave him as a youth. It is one of the highlights of the Christmas season for my grandfather." Words of loving appreciation will also brighten the lives of your partners in Christ who stimulate and strengthen you.

## Partners in Grace

The basis of this Christian partnership is our common experience of God's grace in Jesus Christ. We have all been to Calvary. I have had the privilege of conducting several tours to the Holy Land. Upon our return, we usually have a reunion and reminisce about our experience. Having walked together where Jesus walked has created a bond among us. What held together that little band of 120 who huddled in the upper room after the crucifixion? Was it not their mutual relationship with Christ? If Jesus had never founded the church, Christians would have gravitated together. We have a strong fellow feeling, a common bond, which draws us magnetically into a fellowship. Paul, writing from a lonely prison cell, felt very keenly the loss of that fellowship. He reached out across the miles to verbally join hand and heart with his partners in Christ. Paul's writing not only ministered to the Philippians but also cheered and strengthened him as he reflected upon their love for him. We desperately need each other and frequent interpersonal relationships as Christians to keep the grace of God glowing in our hearts.

An old Scottish minister called one day upon one of his parishioners who had been neglectful in church attendance. They sat down together in front of the fireplace, the parishioner expecting the pastor to rebuke him for his absence. He was like so many today who feel they can be a good Christian without participating in the fellowship. Presently, the pastor took a poker and raked from the fire a glowing coal. For a time, it burned brightly upon the hearth, and then the glow began to fade. Soon, the coal turned cold and black while the fire in the fireplace burned brightly on. The parishioner said, "Pastor, you don't have to say a word. I understand your message."

## Partners in Responsibility

Fellowship in the gospel is not just a getting together but a going together. Christians are bound together not only in common experience but also in common task. Fellowship, then, has a purposeful significance beyond the enjoyment of each other's company. It is the task of sharing the gospel with every person in the world. What happens to a church which loses sight of its mission and puts all the accent upon fellowship? Rigor mortis sets in. Disharmony, disunity, and discontent often plague the church. The membership dwindles away. God takes his blessing from a church that ceases to be a blessing.

The suffering of Paul was lightened by the knowledge that the Philippians were partakers with him in the gospel agonies. Nothing cheers the heart of a pastor more than to have his members step into the battle line with him. Camp followers are a detriment to the church on the march. One is not truly in the fellowship unless he is involved in the ministry of the fellowship. A person might be in the army, but if he has gone AWOL, he is not really a soldier. There is always the temptation as church members to rest on our laurels, to let someone else assume the responsibilities, to support the ministries only in a token fashion, or to let one's energies be absorbed in functions that do not pertain to Christian service.

Mary Crowley, in her book *Think Mink,* expresses great appreciation for a Dallas attorney named Ralph Baker, a deacon in the First Baptist Church. He was very helpful to her in getting her business started. She says that he also taught her a great deal about making the church an important part of her life. Once Ralph filled in as a temporary choir director

at the First Baptist Church while the church was looking for
a professional. When, at last, a minister of music was called,
Mary said to Ralph, "I guess you are going to take a well-earned
rest for awhile." He replied in the negative, indicating he had
already accepted the superintendency of the young marrieds
department. He then explained in a statement which reveals
a significant insight: "I found a long time ago that if you are
not obligated in God's business, the world will take all your
time."

## Partners in Abundant Love

Paul used the strongest expression at his command to con-
vey his loving concern for the Philippians. The love which
he felt for the Philippians was not simply that of an affectionate
friendship. It is a unique kind of love which only Christians
know because it issues from their relationship with Christ. The
ancients felt that the center of love was in the viscera. We
all know how that our emotions affect our internal organs. Paul
felt for the Philippians a deep-seated love akin to that which
Christ reflected in his death upon the cross for us. This is a
love in which we are greatly moved by the needs of our fellow
Christians. It is a love which causes us to become involved in
the lives of our partners in Christ. We cannot stand aloof from
them and watch them struggle or suffer without participating
in their plight.

When Frederick the Great lost by death some of his old
companions, he once said, "I see the only happy people on
earth are those who love nobody." The love of which the apostle
Paul speaks exacts a toll upon us because we identify with
our partners in their conflicts and suffering. Thus, the Philippian Christians agonized with the prisoner Paul, and he, in
turn, longed to be with them that he might share in their
toils and troubles for the gospel's sake.

Paul prayed that the Philippians would abound in an en-
lightened love. It is possible to love unwisely or to display love
in an unintelligent fashion. For example, a little girl has a kitten
which she loves very much. One day, the kitty falls into the

bathtub and gets all wet. The child is distressed but notices that her mother has the oven heated to bake a cake. In her loving concern for the kitten, the child places her kitty in the oven so that it might dry more quickly. She loved well, but not wisely.

Intelligent love does not vent itself just in emotional excess. It is not all sound and fury. It is not just holding hands and singing, "Bless be the tie that binds." There are churches who practice this kind of a Christian love-in, who turn a calloused heart toward certain segments of society. Christian love makes sense only when it reaches out to embrace all humanity.

When the preacher-scientist, Henry Drummond died, D. L. Moody, the evangelist, declared, "Henry Drummond lived in the thirteenth chapter of First Corinthians more than any man I ever knew." This is the chapter which says that a Christian can have many other startling gifts but unless he exhibits love, he is nothing. When King Faruk of Egypt died, a commentator said, "In my book, he rates zero zero." Without love, the Christian is a spiritual cipher. Somebody has said that Christian love knows no horizons. It is love without discrimination or exclusion. In photography, a wide-angle lens has a broad focal range. It can be set so that objects close at hand to infinity are in focus. You might say that Christian love is a wide-angle affair. It encompasses everyone from here to eternity.

## Partners in Moral Discrimination

An intelligent Christian love results in a sensitive conscience. Where love abounds, moral judgments will be more accurate. All of us wrestle with problems of right and wrong. How can we know the difference? Very sincere Christians often are at variance in their understanding of what constitutes moral probity. Is there any test whereby the rightness or wrongness of something can be evaluated? I think Paul would suggest that love is the way to "approve things that are excellent" (v. 10). If every contemplated action is weighed in the light of one's love for Jesus and for his fellowman, this would surely give some insight into its moral character. Today it is extremely urgent that Christians carefully exercise this capacity to discern between right and wrong.

J. C. Penney, the son of a Baptist preacher, started to work at a very early age in order to assist with the family finances. In a store where he was working, he noticed a discrepancy as he looked over the stock. He found that some men's socks were selling at two different prices. Although they were exactly the same in quality, some socks were priced at twenty-five cents a pair and others at two pairs for twenty-five cents. When he mentioned this to the owner of the store, the man became very angry and said to him, "Young man, it is your business to sell, not to establish prices." Penney had been reared according to the strict principles of his preacher father so he resigned his job.

At a later time, J. C. Penney succeeded in establishing his own store which he operated on the principle of the Golden Rule. He sought to infuse this Christian ethic into all of the employees of the giant chain of stores which later operated under his name. Once a salesman approached a businessman in my congregation with a proposition whereby he could make a considerable amount of money. In doing so, he would have to misrepresent things to the public. This Christian businessman replied, "If I've got to make money that way, I'll just go out of business." Where true Christian love prevails, integrity is a more important consideration than affluence, popularity, or a multitude of other things upon which people place priority.

Ecologists are greatly concerned about the pollution of nature. Stringent laws are being passed to protect our environment. It seems rather strange, however, that we, as a people, are concerned so little about the pollution of our minds and souls. As a matter of fact, we seem to be intent today upon the contamination of our inner selves. Pornography, for example, has become a billion dollar business, and our laws seem to be very lenient where these polluting influences are concerned. Movies, magazines, and books deliberately designed to whet our sensual appetites are easily accessible. Some people take the attitude that they can see those movies or read those books without any harm.

This reminds me of a minister who was walking in the shadow of a building that was under construction. He saw a red hot rivet fall from the heights down to a mud puddle where it sizzled and cooled in the dirty water. It occurred to him that this was a parable of life. The person who plunges into the mire of sin loses his spiritual fervor and his life becomes useless to God. One reason people think it is not hurting them to be exposed to this moral trash is because they are becoming desensitized to it, and it no longer seems so bad. Paul was concerned about the corrosive effects of the world upon the Philippian Christians and the consequent destruction of their ability to make moral judgments.

There is always the temptation to evaluate our actions in the light of a consensus of opinion. One of Lincoln's favorite stories was about the farmer who took his son out to the field to teach him to plow. The father advised his son that in order to plow a straight row he should set his eye upon some object at the end of the field and plow toward it. When the farmer returned a bit later, the son had plowed not in a straight line but more like a question mark. He had fixed his eye upon an ox at the end of the field who had moved in the course of his plowing. A person has no fixed standard if he is dependent upon the concepts of a group or of society in general. Christ and our love for him must be the ultimate consideration. It is not old-fashioned to ask, What would Jesus have me to do?

A missionary friend of mine spent many years in the South Pacific. For a long time, he lived alone among some very primitive peoples in the Fiji Islands. He said, "I used to dress for dinner because, you see, I always had to be wary lest I should go native." In this moral jungle we call the world, we also have to be very careful lest we as Christians imitate the lifestyle of the peoples about us. Here again, it is the love of Christ and the positive influence of our fellow Christians which help us resist this tendency to go "native" and live by the distinctive Christian ideals.

## Partners in Righteousness

Churches today are mercilessly under fire. The most articulate criticisms are coming, in many instances, from ministers, themselves. Books are being written analyzing what is wrong with the church. Her creaking, antiquated machinery is being amplified for all to hear. Her sores are being exposed to public gaze. Desperate efforts are being made to pump new blood through the church's corroded arteries. Although it has become popular today to hurl calumnies and criticisms at the church, it would be well to pause and thank God for the church. After all, whatever flaws there are in the church are human. They will be remedied not by abandoning the church, but by renewing our Christian commitment and rethinking our Christian calling.

With its gross inefficiency and obvious faults, the church still stands as a bulwark of Christianity. This is true because in every congregation there is always a core of devout ones who deserve a compliment rather than a scolding. The most adamant critics of the church are usually those who are not doing anything constructive to help the church. Many people think that sluggish churches will become activated by activity. This is something like waving the arms of a corpse in an imitation of life. A church awakens from its slumber by the kiss of spirituality. The Holy Spirit alone can give vitality to a church. The Holy Spirt is given operational liberties only in a congregation of genuinely committed Christians.

It is not criticism but consecration, then, that holds the key to Christian renewal. As partners in righteousness, we are to let the love of Christ in our hearts give free expression in holy living and dedicated service. As a matter of fact, love is something that cannot really be hidden. There is nothing that demands expression more than true love.

One summer when I was a college student, I led a youth revival team over the state of Missouri. A member of that team was the girl who later became my wife. We had already been dating for some time and were very much in love. We felt that it would be unwise, however, during that summer to give any indication that we meant anything to each other. This naturally placed us under a great deal of tension, but we thought we were succeeding. During the third revival on a Wednesday evening, the pastor's wife called us aside after the service. She said, "You two think you're pretty smart, don't you?" She then opened her purse, drew out a set of car keys, and said, "Here, go ride around awhile." In spite of everything, our love had revealed itself.

Living for Jesus is not an onerous thing where there is love. Do you remember that when Jacob had served seven years for Rachel, the woman he loved, it is said, "They seemed unto him but a few days for the love he had for her." Love makes the yoke of Christ easy and our Christian labors a delight. During World War II, reporters sought out the sons of Theodore Roosevelt who were conducting themselves in a very splendid fashion in the European theater of war. When congratulated, one of them replied, "Well, after all, we're the sons of Roosevelt, and we must conduct ourselves correspondingly." As the sons of God, redeemed by his grace in Jesus Christ, with hearts full of love and appreciation, the goals of our lives is the glory of God.

# 9

## Christ's Alter Ego

### PHILIPPIANS 1:12–14,19–26

Max Beerbohm wrote a short story entitled, "The Happy Hypocrite." It is a fable about a very wicked man who fell in love with a pure, chaste young woman. The evil of his life had etched itself into his very countenance. His appearance, as well as his life-style, was repulsive to the girl. Realizing this, he employed the services of a skilled mask maker who carefully covered his face with the mask of a pious and good man. The young woman immediately fell in love with the man whose sterling character shone from his face.

Following their marriage, the evil man sought to live the kind of life which would please his bride and was suggested by his mask. His secret, however, was known by a woman who had shared his wicked life in previous days. Her jealousy was aroused by having been forsaken for another woman, and she determined to expose the hypocrite. One day she accosted him and sank her fingernails into the waxen mask, ripping it from his face.

The man was completely distraught because now he knew he would lose the object of his affection. He was afraid his wife would not be able to tolerate his true countenance. A miracle, however, had transpired in those days when he had worn the mask of a good man and sought to live in that pattern. The features of his face had conformed themselves to the image of the mask. While living like a good man, he had become one.

Companionship with Jesus Christ brings out the very best within us. When we first trust him as our Savior, we have been forgiven of our sins, but we have not become the person Christ intends for us to be. Gradually, as we imitate the pattern of the Lord Jesus Christ, we become conformed into his image.

It was the aspiration of the apostle Paul to so completely commit himself to the Lord Jesus Christ that he might reflect a true image of Christ in himself. His own life situation mattered little as long as through whatever happened to him Christ received glory. Stonewall Jackson expressed the same sentiment to a young theological student who visited him as he lay dying. Said the Christian soldier, "The Christian must carry his religion into everything." He continued to declare that it makes a man "a better commander, a better shoemaker, a better tailor." The more Christlike our lives, the more sterling they are.

No one can realize his full potential apart from identification of himself with Jesus. For it is Jesus who brings out the best within us. John the Baptist said, "He must increase, but I must decrease" (John 3:30). Here is one place where enhancement comes by diminishment. The old ideal, "more of Christ and less of self," is in a sense contrary to experience. The more I give myself to Christ, the more of my self I realize. The commitment of self to Christ does not detract from but rather fulfills and glorifies the self. In Christ, loss is gain.

## Adversity Advertising Christ

Paul, the prisoner, saw his chains as setting off a chain reaction. His imprisonment had been the means of penetrating the palace itself with the gospel. The Castle of Chillon sits sedately on the brink of a lovely lake in Montreux, Switzerland. Down in the dungeon of that castle on one of the pillars is etched the name of Byron. The poet's visit to the castle and the story he learned there inspired his writing "The Prisoner of Chillon." The bonds of Paul were his Byronic spokesman telling of his willingness to live or die for Jesus Christ. Paul's imprisonment was not a waste but a witness and abetted the spread of the gospel.

Adlai Stevenson once declared that the Communists have rediscovered the power to die for what they believe. "This is the reason," he declared, "that they, not we, are firing the shots heard around the world." The early Christians "gloried in tribulation," but, today, we are often chafed by any inconvenience which our faith thrusts upon us. If only we could realize that the trials of life are opportunities to display Christian grace rather than impositions simply to endure.

Christian character sparkles its brightest only under duress of circumstance. If Paul had assumed a martyr's complex and his epistles just capsuled his complaints, what a sad heritage he would have given us. His was the spirit of Christ, "who for the joy set before him endured the cross." Paul would have been willing to suffer any indignity and inconvenience if he thought thereby the gospel would have been furthered.

Mrs. Franklin D. Roosevelt was once making a speech in Los Angeles when a man in the audience shouted, "Mrs. Roosevelt, do you think that being a cripple has affected your husband's mind?" What a cruel question. The first lady seemed to be stunned for a moment, and then she replied that her husband's suffering most certainly had affected his mind. She said that suffering had made him more sensitive and more responsive to his fellowman.

A gifted writer once said to me, "No one is prepared to write poetry who has not suffered." Certainly, the most poetic interpretations of the Christian life I have ever witnessed have been composed by those who have gone through severe trials. It is only in the agonies of life that the full meaning of the Christian hope comes into focus.

## A Magnificent Purpose

I still have in my possession a microscope set which I purchased from a friend when I was about twelve years old. Its magnification is not very powerful, but it opened a whole new world to my startled eyes. I remember one day putting the tiny leg of a bug under the lens and, to my amazement, I saw another infinitesimally small insect crawling on the leg. To the world, generally, Christ is known only by hearsay. He exists historically but not experientially. He is as invisible to most people as that tiny little insect on the bug's leg was to me. Paul's purpose was to magnify Christ in his own body for all to see. It is through us that Christ moves from oblivion to observation where our friends and neighbors are concerned. This startling revelation through our own lives is the only way that the interest of people generally can be aroused to take a look for themselves and discover Christ's reality.

I have a clipping from a newspaper dated Thursday, January 22, 1959. Fidel Castro was leading a revolution in Cuba. The story tells of the spirit of the men who followed him in the overthrow of the Batista government. It says the rebels ignored the hardships and gained strength. An explanation was given by a Captain Torey who said, "When we entered the Rebel Army, we gave ourselves up for dead." These words remind me of a missionary story. When James Calvert went out to the cannibal Fiji Islands to preach the gospel, the captain of the ship on which he was traveling sought to dissuade him. He reminded him that he was going among savages and that surely his life would be lost. Calvert's reply was, "We died before we came." These words are reflective of the spirit of the apostle Paul. Paul placed no premium on his own life. His paramount purpose was to magnify Christ.

I am fully persuaded that there are Christians today who emulate this ideal. They would gladly give their lives, if need be, for the cause of Christ. More important, perhaps Christ and his glory are the primary considerations in their daily living. These are the people who give our churches their spiritual glow. They are positive in their convictions, evident in their witness, consistent in their living, and radiant in their example. They may not live among savages, but, nevertheless, they live and move and have their being in a society which is not generally sympathetic to their Christian ideals. They must absorb the arrows of contempt and endure the blows of blasphemy. They are not intimidated by their minority status or silenced by the verbosity of those who loudly champion evil.

## Christ's Alter Ego

When Robert E. Lee was president of Washington and Lee University, he often took rides with Professor White. As a result, they became very close friend. In later years, however, when Professor White was asked if he had been a confidential friend of Robert E. Lee, he invariably answered, "No Sir, no man was great enough to be intimate with General Lee." The apostle Paul had no such diffidence in talking about his relationship with the one who is greatest of all. As a matter of fact, he thought of himself as Christ's alter ego when he said, "For to me to live is Christ" (v. 21). The words *alter ego* could be translated "other self." The word *alter* literally means "another of the same kind." A person's alter ego is someone with whom he is so closely identified in appearance or in purpose, characteristics, or friendship that to see one is to think of the other. An example of this is found in the relationship between President Woodrow Wilson and his advisor, Colonel House. Wilson constantly sent Colonel House on missions to represent himself. A correspondent once asked Wilson how far Colonel House could speak for him. Wilson replied, "Mr. House is my second personality. He is my independent self. His thoughts and mine are one." [1]

Another example of an alter ego is found in the relationship between President Franklin Roosevelt and Louis McHenry Howe. Howe was a wise and wizened newspaper reporter who associated himself with Roosevelt early in the future president's career. He completely dedicated himself to the fulfillment of Roosevelt's political ambitions. For years, he lived in the Roosevelt home, and he masterminded Roosevelt's political life.

One Roosevelt biographer has said, "After 1912, it would be impossible to think of either Roosevelt or Howe without the other. They operated as parts of one political personality. They complemented each other in strength and weakness— no one would ever be able to write about the twentieth century without mentioning Franklin Delano Roosevelt. No one would be able to write about Roosevelt without mentioning Louis McHenry Howe." [2]

It was with unabashed dedication that Paul submitted his life to Jesus. Our lives, also, should become submerged as far

as possible in the personality of Jesus Christ. We must seek
to think his thoughts and to perform his ministry. Paul empha-
sized the importance of boldness in contrast to embarrassment
in reference to our Christian living. This is to be no clandestine
relationship with Christ. When other people see us, they should
think of Jesus. Our paramount purpose is that of revealing
Jesus through our lives.

The home of D. L. Moody was destroyed in the great Chi-
cago fire. Very few belongings were saved but among them
was a valuable painting of the evangelist. Moody, himself, positively refused to travel through the streets of the burning city
clutching his own portrait. His wife, therefore, cut the canvas
out of the frame, rolled it up, and carried it herself. Moody
was far more concerned about carrying the image of Christ
upon the canvas of his own flesh than an image of himself.

## The Bright Side of Death

Death is like the moon in that it has both a bright side
and a dark side. We can dwell in the shadow of death or live
on its bright side. Christ has so far removed the dark, fearsome
aspect of death that Paul could describe it as "gain." Nothing
so demonstrates the power of God's grace than the fact that
he found a way to turn death into victory. The distinguished
author, Somerset Maugham, said shortly before he died that
he did not believe in an afterlife. He declared that he had
no fear of hell nor did he face "the eternal boredom of heaven."
Perhaps the only acceptable alternative to Christian faith is
cynicism such as this. As far as Christians are concerned,
however, Jesus Christ has validated his promise of life eternal.

One day, Jesus invaded the cemetery and approached the
tomb of a dear friend named Lazarus. Already, death's odor
crept out of the crevices of the tomb because Lazarus had
been dead for four days. Jesus Christ called him back to life
and, thus, punctuated his promise, "I am the resurrection, and
the life: he that believeth in me, though he were dead, yet

shall he live" (John 11:25). Some of his critics probably said this was a prearranged hoax, but then a bit later, Jesus Christ in the presence of a multitude of gaping spectators died on the cross.

Jesus' death was confirmed by the thrust of a spear into his heart. His body was reverently released from the nails that pinioned it to the cross and wrapped in grave clothes and placed in a new tomb. A contingency of soldiers kept a twenty-four-hour vigil at the entrance of the sealed tomb. Every precaution was taken against any subterfuge, chicanery, or hocus-pocus. In spite of it all, when the stone mysteriously rolled away from the tomb, it was found to be empty. For forty days thereafter, Jesus gave his apostles, and on one occasion above five hundred people, an opportunity to see him alive. Here was proof positive.

To each succeeding generation of believers, Christ presents himself alive. In a sense, he came to me as realistically one night at the age of twelve as he did to Mary Magdalene on the morning of his resurrection. How do we discern his presence today? Remember the words of the two men whom Christ joined on the road to Emmaus. They did not at first recognize him but later remarked, "Did not our heart burn within us, while he talked with us by the way?" (Luke 24:32) This burning of the heart was my experience, too. God's presence was noted by Moses in a burning bush. God makes his presence known when he sets our hearts aflame.

It was on the basis of his relationship with the living Christ that Paul could say, "to die is gain" (v. 21). He had in mind the promise of Christ who said, "that where I am, there ye may be also" (John 14:3). In what respect is death gain? It is gain inasmuch as death ushers the Christian into the more immediate presence of Jesus Christ. Paul said, "This is far better." In other words, death becomes an advantage. There is nothing supremely good in this life which we do not have more of in heaven. What appears to be loss is actually gain. It is like going to sleep bankrupt and waking up a billionaire. Christ turns death's deficit into our most valuable asset.

## I'll Live till I Die

One of Victor Hugo's characters said, "It is nothing to die. It's an awful thing never to have lived." He meant by this that many people do not really live, they simply expend their days. Life is something to be used up, not something to be utilized for high and holy purposes. The oldest recorded person was Methuselah who lived to be 969 years of age. The Bible says, "He was born, he begat, and he died." He had nearly a thousand years to make a contribution worth remembering but, evidently, he goofed it away. Someone has said that man is the only creature who knows he is going to die. This is a tremendous advantage to us because it presses upon us the urgency of making our life count. Woodrow Wilson was once warned that he might be assassinated. He replied, "I am immortal until my time comes." He was raised in a Presbyterian preacher's home and had strong feelings that his life and death were preordained. I doubt that many of us really believe that. Otherwise, we would not get all concerned about health fads. We wouldn't be so intent upon taking care of ourselves. Safety belts in our cars would be foolish. We are a little like the Pilgrim who maintained the doctrine of predestination. One day he took his gun from the rack and announced to his wife that he was going through the woods to a neighbor's house. His wife asked him why he was taking his gun since he believed in the doctrine of predestination. "Well," replied the Pilgrim, "I might meet an Indian, and it would be his time to die, and I wouldn't have my gun."

We are probably born with a biological time clock which we have inherited from our ancestors. Under normal circumstances, we each have a certain life expectancy. Longevity is inherited among other things. We also know that medical science has made significant strides in increasing life expectancy. We have a far better chance of growing old than did our predecessors. In fact, one elderly person said, "Doctors won't let us die short of suicide, and theologians won't let us commit suicide with peace of mind."

We are all going to live until we die, but how we live and for what purpose are important considerations. The purpose of Paul's life was to glorify Christ. There is a sense in which every Christian is called to reincarnate the life of Christ. Paul had only one regret at dying. He felt that he was still needed and that his mission was not complete.

P. T. Barnum was the fabulous impresario of last century who amassed a fortune through deceit and hokum. When he was in his final illness, he wondered what the newspapers would say of him after he was gone. *The Evening Sun* of New York learned of this and asked permission to publish his obituary in advance so that he might enjoy it. The permission was granted, and Barnum reveled in the headline, "Great and Only Barnum. He wanted to read his obituary. Here it is."

How would you like your obituary to read? Paul wrote his own obituary with these simple but magnificent words, "For to me to live is Christ, and to die is gain." The word *eulogy* is offensive to some people because of its association with flattering and flowery remarks spoken over the dead. Paul's remark was not an embellishment nor an egotistic self-eulogy. It was a forthright declaration of the purpose of his life. What similarity might there be with an honest obituary you and I might pen of our lives?

Beneath the altar of the Church of Saint Paul Outside the Walls in Rome, a light glows identifying, we are told, the place where Paul was buried. Tradition has it that Paul was beheaded on the Ostian Way. The circumstances of one's death and the disposal of his body are not nearly so important, however, as the manner of his life. The influence of Paul's life abides with us today and continues with us for our "furtherance and joy of faith."

### Notes

1. Henry M. Wriston, "The Special Envoy," Foreign Affairs (January, 1960), p. 223.

2. Alfred B. Rollins, Jr., *Roosevelt and Howe* (New York: Alfred A. Knoff, 1962), pp. 61, 449.

# 10

## One in the Spirit

PHILIPPIANS 1:27–28; 2:1–11

When I sit quietly and listen to the sounds out of my past, one that comes to me very distinctly is the ringing of the church bell on Sunday morning calling our community to worship. To some of us, it was the voice of joy because, like the psalmist, we could say, "I was glad when they said unto me, Let us go into the house of the Lord" (122:1). For others, it was an irritating sound jangling their nerves, arousing them from their Sunday morning lethargy, and tingling their consciences a bit.

For a while my oldest brother, then a teenager, had the job of ringing the church bell on Sunday. As a little boy, I was delighted when he would let me hold the rope with him and help him ring the bell. In essence, this symbolizes the spirit of Christian fellowship. We are taking hold of the rope together to ring out the joyous news of Jesus and his love. It is also important that we pull together if the music of the bell is to resound across the world.

One day a blind boy was taking a walk along a familiar pathway near the school he was attending. Another boy and his dog rushed by, brushing against the blind boy and knocking him into the bushes. When he arose, he had lost his sense of direction. He didn't know which way to go. He shouted for help, but no one heard him. Presently, he heard the chimes in the steeple of the chapel. Then he knew the right direction and returned along the pathway. The spiritually blind are stumbling about in confusion. They are lost and bewildered, feeling their way hopefully toward some unknown destiny where they will find meaning, hope, and security. We who know Christ are the bell ringers of mankind. Through our witness alone can people find their way home.

In Corpus Christi, Texas, where I live, the backyards of many homes are surrounded by board fences. This makes for privacy but often for poor relations with neighbors. A few years ago when the city was struck by Hurricane Celia, there was great devastation and most of those board fences were blown down. Neighbors who had merely spoken previously got together and helped each other. Our world is in a state of spiritual emergency. If there were no other reason for Christians uniting, the plight of humanity should be enough. There are cultural, economic, racial, and temperamental barriers between Christians, but these will come down and Christians will get together in the common cause of rendering spiritual assistance to people in trouble if the love of Christ is in our hearts.

## One in Resolute Purpose

The word *together* has a very strong emotional content. It is in the arena of togetherness that we have our most meaningful experiences. In speaking of marriage, the Bible says, "What God hath joined together" (Matt. 19:6). Poetically, we speak with rapture about the bliss of solitude, but, actually, life would be a very drab affair apart from our loving relationships. A businessman was being honored at a banquet. In his response, he expressed gratitude for the kind tributes, but, then, he added, "It really doesn't mean all that much to me now, for, you see, a year ago my wife died and I have nobody to tell it to." All of the distinctive qualities of the human being, his personality, ability to communicate, capacity for love, and the like, suggest that life was meant for sharing and in this context we receive our greatest satisfactions.

The church is one of the most rewarding outlets for this instinct of togetherness. Just as in marriage, the church is constituted of people whom God hath joined together. If the togetherness is real, there will be a similarity in life-style of church members. They will share a common purpose, and they will work together toward its achievement. The unifying factor in the church is the devotion to Christ and his gospel.

There is a great variety of opinion as to what constitutes

acceptable Christian behavior. Even as I write, the attention of the nation has been focused upon a popular entertainer named Anita Bryant who has taken a public stand against a measure which would make it illegal to discriminate against homosexuals in her home county. She is a devoted Christian and bases her position, in part, upon her understanding of Christian ideals. On the other hand, there have been established in recent years a few churches with members and pastors who openly confess themselves as gay.

To drink or not to drink is also a very live issue when Christians discuss morality. Many years ago, I was on a train traveling to Texas, and the woman who sat next to me soon discovered that I was a young Baptist minister. She confessed that she and her husband had once been Baptists but had forsaken the fold to join another denomination which did not frown on drinking. She said that in recent days she had attended a cocktail party at which her present pastor was also a guest and participated in the drinking. With some indignation, she said, "I don't think that is right. Somebody should hold the line."

Actually, all of us as Christians have the responsibility of holding the line where proper behavior is concerned. There may be individual differences of opinion about what is right and what is wrong, but we do have a guideline. Paul said that our behavior should be as "it becometh the gospel of Christ" (v. 27). Personal preference is beside the point. What really matters is whether our behavior is consistent with our Christian commitment. This principle applies whether we are pastors in the pulpit or parishioners in the pew.

Of course, this kind of a stand takes a great deal of personal courage and dedication. If we are not careful, we will be intimidated into compromise by those who do not share our Christian ideals. They have a tendency to resent our idealism but then will ridicule the Christian when he fails to live up to it. There is no way a Christian can win in trying to conciliate his worldly friends. When he compromises, he ends up with their contempt and the burden of a guilty conscience. But, after all, the true soldier is not intent upon obtaining the applause of the enemy but the commendation of his commander.

One of the purposes of the church, of course, is that we might encourage each other in living for Jesus. When Christians stand together, they are not so likely to fall. The secret of Alexander the Great's victories was the phalanx. His soldiers marched together in tight units. They bore long shields and spears. The men in front held their shields before them as they approached the enemy. The soldiers behind held their shields above their heads and, thus, were protected from the arrows of the enemy. They marched straight-forward in a solid mass and no army could withstand them. When Christians march together in unity, they protect each other and also constitute a formidable force for good in the world.

## One in Loving Fellowship

Paul, in chapter 2:1–2, piled up a lot of love words. In his letters when he wanted to make a strong point, he fired a verbal barrage of words that reveal facets of his idea. Notice how he arrayed such love words as *consolation, comfort, fellowship*. Down in verse 2, there is an expression which summarizes what he had in mind. Williams has translated the words, "being of one accord," like this: "Your hearts beating in unison." When Christians' hearts are beating together, their minds will be together. They will be operating on the same spiritual wavelength. When their thoughts are together, they can act in unison. Gone will be the petty jealousies, the silly differences, the awkward divisiveness which often plague churches. Without love, the mind becomes prideful and vainglorious. When a person's heart is not right, he often becomes a headache to the church. He would rather argue than agree. He would rather criticize than commend. He would rather gripe than give. Dissolving of differences in the church family is usually a matter of getting hearts right with God.

James Irwin in his book *To Rule The Night* tells of his religious experience in association with his flight into space. He had accepted Christ as a boy of eleven at a revival meeting but had not stayed close to the Lord. After his flight into space, he had the growing feeling that God had a mission for him. Furthermore, prior to the flight, he and his wife had been having some differences which threatened to destroy their home. After renewing his relationship with Christ, the picture changed, and Irwin said, "Our old differences have paled. It is happening very simply because when you know Jesus Christ, differences fade away." The love of Christ is the great amalgamator. When Christian love prevails in a church, the differences seem trifling. The Holy Spirit is able to knit the congregation into a holy partnership.[1]

This tie of Christian love which binds us together is very real. Christians feel a kinship with other Christians whenever and wherever they meet. On a visit to Russia, I found the people, generally speaking, unsmiling and distant. But at the Baptist church in Moscow, it was different. Here, we were greeted heartily and embraced with Christian love. The barriers of nationality, language, and ideology were overcome by the feeling of oneness in Christ. I was reminded of an article in the newspaper some years ago about a visit to Russia by some American diplomats. A reporter accompanying the group remarked, "The only happy people I saw in Russia were in the Baptist church in Moscow."

## One in Humble Obedience

The humility of Jesus was complete. He came from heaven's glory to earth's grief, from heaven's majesty to earth's misery. He came from deity to dust, from King to slave. Although he was God, he condescended to become a man and the humblest of men, at that. The Jews had expected the Messiah to come in his regality. They could not conceive of him being born in a peasant home, making his living by an ordinary trade. There were no royal robes for Jesus, just the plain garments of the working man, sweat stained, homespun, and perhaps patched. There were no rings on his fingers, but caluses on his hands. There was no red carpet, but a rugged path of toil and tribulation. There was no throne, but a cross. The humility of Jesus reflected itself finally in his obedience to the death of the cross. He who was holy God condescended to die like an accursed criminal. This was the descent and humiliation of Jesus.

It is this mind of humility and obedience that Paul asked us to emulate. Humility is a subtle quality that is difficult to identify. How do we know whether we are humble? If we think we are humble, in all likelihood, we are not. Genuine humility probably reflects itself best through eager obedience.

Adoniram Judson's report of his call and surrender to missionary service is a good example of the attitude Paul is talking about. Judson says, "It was during a solitary walk in the woods behind the college while meditating and praying on the subject and feeling half inclined to give it up that the command of Christ, 'Go into all the world and preach the gospel to every creature,' was presented to my mind with such clearness and power that I came to a full decision, and though great difficulties appeared in my way, resolved to obey the command at all events." [2] In contrast to the attitude of Judson is that reflected by a church member who heard that Ann Hasseltine, Judson's fiancee, had made a similar commitment. The woman commented to a friend, "I hear that Miss Hasseltine is going to India. Why does she go?"

Her friend replied, "She thinks it her duty. Would you not go if you thought it your duty?"

The reply came back, "But I would not think it my duty." [3]

The secret of humility, apparently, is to have a mind of obedience. Obedience, I believe, is the key to spiritual growth and depth. Trying to be humble is an awkward exercise. Obedience, on the other hand, is something very tangible by which we can discipline our lives. We know immediately some of the things Christ wants us to be and to do. He wants us to live clean, pure lives. He wants us to be faithful church members. He expects us to be good stewards. He intends for us to witness. I need go no further because obedience in these things would put us well on the road to humility.

A young college girl was touring the home of Beethoven.

Upon seeing Beethoven's piano, before anyone could stop her, she slipped under the rope and began to play the instrument. She said to the custodian, "I suppose every musician who comes here wants to play this piano." He told her that recently the world renowned pianist, Paderewski, had visited Beethoven's home and someone had asked him to play the piano. He had replied, "No, I do not feel worthy to play the great master's piano."

We can never expect to reflect the same quality of humble obedience which Jesus displayed in his death upon the cross. We can, however, offer his Gethsemane prayer, "Not as I will but as thou wilt" (Matt. 26:39) and sincerely seek to imitate his life of obedience.

When Anne Sullivan became the teacher of blind and deaf Helen Keller, she found the six-year-old girl completely unmanageable. Miss Sullivan came to realize that it was useless to try to teach Helen language or anything else until she learned to obey. Miss Sullivan later remarked that she had become persuaded by the experience that obedience is the gateway through which knowledge and love enter the mind of a child. I feel that this is a valid principle in the Christian life. The blessings of God are received by the Christian in proportion to his obedience to the will of God. One of the paramount characteristics of Christ, Paul said, was that of obedience. It is the very essence of humility.

## One in Allegiance to the King of Kings

Christians should be united in their open confession of Jesus Christ as Lord of lords and King of kings. I remember that Jesus asked, "Why call ye me Lord, Lord, and do not the things which I say?" (Luke 6:46). The only acceptable confession is one which expresses itself daily in allegiance to him who is above all. Our lives must be oriented to him as a sailor is to the North Star. The direction of our lives will be determined by our love for and loyalty to Jesus Christ.

A 1977 newspaper announced that soon a book is to be published which contains the contributions of several theological professors who deny the deity of Jesus Christ. How sad that some of the most blatant denigrations of Jesus come from the lips and the pens of persons who claim to be Christians. The detractors of Christ have been legion from the very beginning. What is the answer to their learned propositions? It is the fidelity of the faithful. It is the testimony of those who have enthroned Christ in their hearts.

One of the most significant witnesses to the lordship of Christ in recent days is the book by Charles Colson, *Born Again.* Charles Colson was known as President Nixon's hatchet man. He reached out from his position of power next to the president to destroy those on the White House enemy list. To him, Christ was an institution, not a living reality. It was a name to employ in his epithets. But then came the disastrous day when he was toppled from his flimsy pinnacle, his ambitions demolished, his future in shambles. In this time of despair, he came under the influence of a handful of Christian men, some of whom had been on the White House enemy list. Through them, Colson learned that Christ is alive and on his throne but not so remote that he will not reach out in compassion to every needy person. Colson's life was dramatically changed by the power of Christ. This man who once conceived diabolical schemes for hurting people has dedicated himself to the ministry of helpfulness in the name of Christ.

This year (1977) the British are celebrating the Silver Anniversary of Queen Elizabeth's reign. In my files I have an article from a 1952 copy of the *Readers' Digest* entitled, "England Prepares to Crown a Queen." It describes the pageantry and the protocol of her coming coronation. I happened to be in London a short time before her investment and saw the bleachers erected along the streets and the dressing up of Westminster Abbey, the site of the coronation. The article from *Readers' Digest* quotes the invitation which the Queen sent to her peers:

"Right Trusty and Well-Beloved Cousin. We greet You Well. Whereas We have appointed the Second Day of June, 1953, for the Solemnity of our Coronation, these are therefore to will and command You, all Excuses set apart, that You make your personal attendance upon Us, at the time above mentioned, furnished and appointed as to your Rank and Quality appertaineth, there to do and perform such Services as shall be required." [4]

The wording of this invitation leaves no room for ambivalence or alternative. Neither does the call of Christ. He said, "If ye love me, keep my commandments" (John 14:15). Allegiance to Christ is inevitable for those who sincerely trust and love him.

An American soldier was riding on a train in North Dakota. Somehow, he lost his ticket and the conductor demanded cash fare. The soldier drew out his wallet to obtain the money. The conductor noticed, however, that in the wallet the man carried a miniature of Sallman's head of Christ. He looked at the boy and said, "If you carry that picture, Son, you must be telling the truth. Just keep your money."

Hopefully, through the testimony of lives of Christian integrity, the world will come to realize that we bear in our hearts the image of the living Christ.

### Notes

1. James B. Irwin with William A. Emerson, Jr., *To Rule the Night* (Philadelphia: A. J. Holeman Company, 1973), p. 250.

2. Courtney Anderson, *To the Golden Shore* (Boston: Little, Brown, and Co., 1956), pp. 56–57.

3. Ibid., p. 85.

4. Rene Lecler, "England Prepares to Crown a Queen," *Readers' Digest* (December, 1952), p. 26.

# 11

## A Sparkling Christian

PHILIPPIANS 2:14–30

When Shirley Temple was a child star, she captured the hearts of the American people as perhaps no one else ever has. I have read that when she was performing before the camera, her mother would stand to one side and keep mouthing the words, "Sparkle, Shirley, sparkle." In the instance of the Philippian Christians, the apostle Paul was their spiritual mentor standing just off stage and saying to them, "Sparkle for Jesus." He told them that they were to "shine as lights in the world." *Today's English Version* has an interesting translation of these words: "You must shine among them like stars lighting up the sky" (v. 15).[1] In other words, Christians are to be spiritual luminaries. Every person who is born again becomes a star in the night sky of this world. Each Christian is like a cheerful pin prick of light in the foreboding darkness of evil. Paul was simply echoing the instruction of Jesus who said, "Let your light so shine before men, that they may see . . ." (Matt. 5:16). John Masefield talked about needing a "star to steer by." Christians are to provide a moral and spiritual example for those who walk in darkness.

### An Energy Crisis

Is your life as lustrous as it should be? Most of us would have to confess that our performance is something less than sparkling. This is true, in some instances, because of an energy shortage. I had the privilege of knowing and preaching the funeral of a man who was called the prophet of the oil age. His name was Patillo Higgins, an eccentric, one-armed man who became convinced there was oil at Spindletop Springs outside of Beaumont, Texas. The state geologist insisted that there was no oil on the Texas Coast. Nevertheless, for ten year Higgins sought to interest people in drilling at Spindletop. Some did, but they were equipped only to drill a few hundred feet.

Finally, the Hammel brothers with great ingenuity responded to the appeal of Patillo Higgins. They thrust their drills deep into the earth and a gusher came forth, the first of modern times. Previously, an oil field was considered very productive if it provided a few hundred barrels a day. In the gusher-type well, thousands and thousands of barrels of oil were available. It was discoveries like Spindletop that made the oil age possible. For several decades, we pretended that the supply of oil was inexhaustible. What a shock it is to find ourselves in an energy crisis.

An energy crisis is nothing new for Christians. We are experiencing a constant drain of spiritual energy in the effort to live by the Christian ideal. When we accepted Christ as Savior, it was like the gusher at Spindletop. We were infused with spiritual energy and enthusiastically set about living for Jesus. If we have not across the years continued to drill new wells, the supply from that initial experience gets rather thin. Finally, we have to confess like the foolish virgins, "We have no oil. Our lamps are gone out" (see Matt. 25:1–12).

The supply of spiritual energy is inexhaustible. It is our failure to constantly tap the supply which results in our shortage. In verse 13, Paul said, "It is God which worketh in you both to will and to do of his good pleasure." The words "worketh in" come from a Greek word which we have brought over into English as "energize." Paul was literally saying, "It is God who energizes you." All energy for moral and spiritual power comes from God. Here is a great pool of power accessible to us if we really want it. Don't you get a little weary going through life like a twenty-five watt bulb when God meant you to be a brilliant spotlight? Don't you get a little ashamed of giving off the spiritual warmth of a match when God meant you to be a blazing campfire? There may have been a time when you were a more zealous and fervent Christian than now, but something has happened along the way.

When Hurricance Celia struck Corpus Christi, the electric line from our house to the light pole blew down. We were completely without power. Our next-door neighbors, however, did not lose their electrical line. Consequently, their power was restored much sooner than ours. They permitted us to run a long extension cord from their house to ours so that we could at least operate our refrigerator. In many instances, some of us, perhaps, have lost our connection with the real source of power and we are living off somebody else's power. We don't have a direct line to God.

Without having been there, it is almost impossible to imagine the horror into which New York City was cast by the recent blackout. Evil, which was held somewhat in check by the light, emerged in the darkness with subsequent looting, pillage, and violence. I believe that the principle thing which restrains the powers of darkness in the world today is the light of Christianity. The influence of churches and of individual Christians extends out into the world, making a wholesome impact in behalf of good. When Christians fail to shine, however, society suffers and evil flourishes.

Christians can lose their first love, their first joy, their first enthusiasm, their first power. This happens when the cares of the world, temptations, and other interests crowd in. We may come to that point in which we cannot take much real interest in the church, Bible study, prayer, or witnessing. We are in a spiritual brownout.

Sometime ago, I was having difficulty with my electric razor. It is the kind which when not in use rests on a charger so that I simply lift it off the charger and can use it without a cord. The razor, however, began to run down and would stop in the middle of a shave. It was not properly energized. I began to investigate and found that I was not actually pushing my razor far enough down onto the charger. It was not making a good connection and, therefore, was not receiving the power from the source. To correct the energy shortage in our lives so that we may be fully utilized by God as lights in the world, we must be sure to have a good connection. A more firm commitment to the Lord and his will is the initial step in restoring the illumination of our lives.

Paul suggested also that illumination comes from the elimination of anything unworthy in our lives. One day, my automobile went dead on the street of our city. A mechanic from a nearby filling station came and took a look. He found that the battery cables were corroded. He explained that this corrosion acted as a resistor and prevented the power from the battery getting through. Moral and spiritual corrosion is also a resistor and until we get our lives cleaned up, the power of God can't flow through.

Another suggestion to rekindle the sparkle in our lives is that of "holding forth the word of life" (v. 16). The purpose of light is to share itself. If we are not busy witnessing for Jesus and sharing the word of life, then what reason does God have to energize us? God exercises a strict economy where divine energy is concerned. He bestows it only where it is going to be utilized. The more active you become in his service, the greater will be the supply of power.

### Smile, You're on Candid Camera

Photography is one of my hobbies. I find that it is very difficult to obtain a natural pose of a subject. Usually, I end up with a self-conscious grin. Furthermore, I have found it is almost impossible to please someone with a picture of themselves. What I feel is a good likeness, they will declare doesn't look like them at all. Sometimes I want to respond like the photographer who was told by a woman, "That picture doesn't do me justice."

He replied, "Lady, what you need is not justice but mercy."

I think most of us have an idealized image of ourselves which does not conform to reality, and this is why we are not usually pleased with our own photographs. Furthermore, we try to project this idealized image to others. We want them to see us not as we are but as we would like to be. This is why candid photography is so devastating. There is no opportunity to pose or to pretend. I certainly would not want pictures being made of me in some of those awkward moments when I am just being myself. Nevertheless, whether I like it or not, everywhere I go people have their cameras aimed toward me. They are constantly forming candid impressions of who I am and what I am like. No one is a good enough actor to completely conceal their true self from these probing cameras.

Pope John, the genial pontiff of the Roman Catholic Church, was constantly besieged for his protrait. He once said, "The good Lord knew from all eternity I would become Pope. Wouldn't you think he could have made me a little more photogenic?" An early Christian work entitled, "St. Paul and Thecla," provides us a not very flattering image of Paul. He is described as a man of small stature, partly bald, crooked legs, eyes set close together, and a hook nose. Not very photogenic, I would say. His life, on the other hand, was a thing of beauty.

Fortunately, for some of us, physiognomy is not as important with God as spirituality. One of the most beautiful aspects of Paul's life was his willingness to suffer without complaint. The candid camera never caught Paul sitting around moping in self-pity. He never played upon the sympathy of his readers. He was ready to pay whatever price was necessary to fulfill his calling.

Someone will remind me of Paul's thorn in the flesh which he asked God three times to remove. I believe this thorn in the flesh was some physical problem which Paul felt handicapped his ministry. When the Lord did not see fit to remove the thorn, Paul did not pout. Paul was not a masochist. I do not think that he enjoyed the beatings, the shipwrecks, the stonings, and the imprisonments. Nevertheless, he did not resent them but took it all in stride as one of the hazards in Christian service.

## Christ Is Number One

The sparkling Christian is one who puts Christ first in his life. Paul portrayed Timothy as a Christian who had subordinated himself to Jesus Christ. Nothing meant more to Timothy than the cause of Christ. This does not mean, for example, that the Christian businessman must neglect his business or be less efficient. It means that he will commit his business to Jesus Christ and not let Christ take a back-seat to his material pursuits. One evening last year President and Mrs. Jimmy Carter spent the night in the home of Mr. and Mrs. Owen Cooper of Yazoo City, Mississippi. A televised newscast showed the Coopers busily making last-minute preparations for the coming of their distinguished guests. It is an exciting and historic event to play host to the president of the United States.

Many years ago, I preached in a revival meeting at the First Baptist Church, Yazoo City. At that time, I became acquainted with the Coopers and was a guest for a meal in their home. I became aware of the fact that a permanent guest in the Cooper home was One more distinguished than the president. Mr. Cooper was already a very successful business executive, but, at the same time, it was very plain that Jesus Christ had the priority in his life. As time went by, the denomination recognized the unique spiritual quality of this Christian businessman and elected him as president of the Southern Baptist Convention.

One of the great inconsistencies evident in most of our lives is the fact that we proclaim Christ as Lord but serve him with reservations. We sing, "Have thine own way, Lord," with our fingers crossed. Charles Fuller, who preached for so many years on the "Old-Fashioned Revival Hour," was converted after he was a grown man and already married. Immediately, the focus of his life changed from that of getting ahead in the business world and making money to the service of the Lord. He wrote a letter to his wife in which he said, "There has come a complete change in my life. I feel now I want to serve God. If he can use me, instead of making the goal of my life the making of money, I may have a call to go to the mission field in Africa."

Mrs. Fuller found herself confronted with a new situation. She had not married a preacher but a businessman, but now she found herself on the verge of becoming a missionary. I'll go with him anywhere in the world, she thought, but, oh my goodness, I hope it isn't to a hot climate.[2]

Although the Lord did not send Charlie Fuller in person to Africa, he and his wife went through some hard and "hot" times while getting his ministry started. She stood by him through thick and thin as he launched a worldwide radio ministry which led thousands to Christ.

## A Calculated Risk

Paul offered Epaphroditus as another example of the sparkling Christian. Paul piled up many compliments and concluded his characterization by indicating that Epaphroditus risked his life in the service of Christ. Christianity is a calculated risk because it is staking everything on Jesus. The person who accepts Christ has placed his life and eternal destiny at the feet of Jesus. In gambling terms, it is an all or nothing-at-all throw of the dice. If Christianity is a farce, then he has made a fatal mistake. If Christ is all he claims to be, he is a winner beyond his imagination. The perils of the Christian life are nothing compared with the rewards.

There is a kind of reckless abandon about the life of a true Christian. He will venture into the unknown, believing that God will lead him. He will assume impossible tasks, convinced he can accomplish them by the power of the Holy Spirit. He may tithe his income, though he doesn't know where next month's rent is coming from. He becomes expendable, placing no priority upon his personal comfort and security but everything upon what he feels to be the will of God. He runs the risk of being misunderstood, disliked, and misused because of his convictions. He may be criticized and ostracized even among his own kin. From time to time, he must ask himself, Is it worth it all?

Robert Louis Stevenson was looking through a scrapbook one day which his mother had kept across the years. In it were notices about her famous son from the newspaper, reviews of his books, and the like. A friend asked him jestingly, "Is fame all it's cracked up to be?"

Stevenson replied, "Yes, when I see my mother's face." The risks of the road will all seem worthwhile when we get to the end of the journey and see our Master's face.

The Christian is exceedingly fortunate because he has associated his life with something preeminently worthwhile. One of the astronauts was asked why he would engage in such a dangerous journey. He replied, "It's a chance to pioneer on a grand scale. It is a chance for immortality. This is something I would give my life for." Christians have found something worth dying for. The service of Jesus infuses their lives with purpose and meaning. They are caught up in a cause that is ultimate in its significance. Their lives are not spent groveling with trifles but dealing with destiny.

It is the vacuity of life that catches up with many people and fills them with despair. Billy Graham once asked for a conference with Marilyn Monroe when he heard she was not well. He had hoped to give her some spiritual guidance and telephoned her home for an appointment. The request was turned down. A few weeks before her death, she ate at a well-known Newport Beach restaurant. In the travel guest book she scribbled her name in the appropriate place. For home address, she wrote, "no place," and in the space allotted for destination, she wrote, "nowhere" and underlined it.

The whole country was shocked by the suicide of Freddie Prinz, a young man who seemed to have everything going for him. He was a huge success at the age of nineteen when be became a part of a popular television series. He had money, glamor, and acclaim, yet, he put a pistol to his head and pulled the trigger. Some blamed the breakup of his marriage for his distress, but thousands of people have their marriages break up without committing suicide. One of his friends in analyzing the situation said, "Something was missing."

A few years ago, a young woman committed suicide leaving behind a note which read, "A year ago I made a bargain with God, or fate, or something in which I said if I did not find something worth living for within the next year I would quit living. I did not find it." She didn't find it because she didn't look for it in the right place. She was waiting for life to dump in her lap an exciting purpose.

People can bear almost anything except meaninglessness. We are so constituted that we must have some rhyme and reason in our life, even if it is very trivial. A child once defined *vacuum* as "a big empty place where the Pope lives." The most miserable people on earth are those who try to live in a big empty place. Somebody has well said that the happiest people are those who have associated their lives with some well-defined good as opposed to some deeply scorned evil. If this be true, then Christians should certainly be the most happy people in existence. They should actually sparkle with the joy of life.

One of the most familiar faces to the American public is the genial countenance of Colonel Sanders of fried chicken fame. Late in life, Colonel Sanders made an astonishing success with his special formula for frying chicken. All of his life, Colonel Sanders had tried to be a useful citizen. Even though he was not a Christian, he gave a tithe to the church. He says, "I was a good Rotarian and tried to live by the Four-Way Test. I was a good citizen and all of that. But all this while, I knew I wasn't right with God. It bothered me especially when I would take the name of the Lord in vain." When he was seventy-nine years of age, he gave his heart to the Lord Jesus Christ. In his testimony he says, "When I walked out of the church that night, I knew I was a different man. I had met God like I had never met him before. All my tithing and good deeds had never given me the sense of God's presence that I knew then, and that feelin' has never left me." [3]

Living for Jesus brought into Col. Sanders' life a new dimension of happiness. He has devoted his time, energy, and money to the cause of Christ. In his homespun way, he offers a sage bit of advice when he says, "Like I often say, there's no use in bein' a religious man when you're lyin' in a cemetery. If you're gonna do anything for God, do it while you're still alive." [4]

### Notes

1. This quotation is from *The Bible in Today's English Version*. Old Testament: Copyright © American Bible Society 1976. New Testament: Copyright © American Bible Society 1966, 1971, 1976. Used by permission.

2. Daniel P. Fuller, *Give the Winds a Mighty Voice* (Waco, Texas: Word Books, 1972), pp. 34–35.

3. Harland Sanders, *Finger Lickin' Good* (Carol Stream, Illinois: Creation House, 1974), pp. 136–141.

4. Ibid., p. 70.

# 12

## How to Be a Good Winner

PHILIPPIANS 3:4–14

One of the hardest things in all the world is to be a good loser. I don't like to lose at anything. When I was playing basketball, I played to win. It was no particular consolation when people said to us following a loss, "You put up a good fight. You can't win them all." The fact remained that we had lost. We might politely go over and congratulate our opponents, but down in our hearts there was a deep sense of disappointment.

Bill Glass, who grew up here in Corpus Christi, Texas, played defensive end for the Cleveland Browns football team. He is a great big hulk of a fellow who is now devoting his time to the preaching of the gospel. When he was playing football, he was sometimes asked to talk to a group of high school students about being good losers. His reply was that he had no material on that subject. He could tell them how to conduct themselves after a loss but said he could not tell them how to be good losers. "It is too easy for a good loser to keep losing," he said.

Paul expounded the proposition in this passage, however, that the Christian in order to be a good winner must first of all know how to be a good loser. The object of the game called Christianity is to "win Christ," as Paul said. Christianity is one game in which every participant is a winner. There is a difference, however, in being a winner and a good winner. There are those who just barely eke out a victory by meeting the minimal requirements of becoming a Christian. They are saved, so to speak, by the skin of their teeth. Others go on to become real Christian champions. What makes the difference? For one thing, Paul said it is the willingness upon the part of the participant to lose, or forfeit, those things which stand between him and "the excellency of the knowledge of Christ Jesus."

## Sacrificing Self-Confidence

Paul suffered a severe blow to the solar plexus when he was brought to his knees on the Damascus Road. It was a severe ego shock to this proud Pharisee when he was made to realize that he was a chump rather than a champ. He must have spent those three days of Damascus darkness in a gloomy wrestling match with his own pride. He had gloried in his degrees and pedigrees. He had felt that he was scoring points with God by persecuting the church. On a scale of one to ten, Paul rated himself a ten as a religious man. His score: "Blameless."

I heard about a newlywed couple who were determined that they would solve their problems without fighting. They put up a complaint box, and if one of them noticed anything about the other which was irritating and might make for trouble in the future, he was to write a note about it and put it in the box. From time to time, the husband and wife were to go the box alone, take out the notes with his or her name on it, read the notes, and do their best to change. At the end of the year, they were discussing their marvelous invention for a happy home but discovered that neither one had ever opened the complaint box. Each one had been so certain that he or she was innocent of all fault that neither had looked in the box.

Paul's profession of blamelessness was before he met Jesus. In the glare of the holy light which struck him blind on the Damascus Road, he was able to see something he had never before realized. He was a proud, arrogant, and condemned sinner. In those hours that followed, he surrendered all confidence in himself and his heritage and his own righteousness. In return, he gained Christ. He suddenly realized that all those things he had valued so highly were nothing but spiritual garbage in contrast to the surpassing worth of knowing Christ as Savior.

Kyle Rote, Jr., came to the attention of the American people as a successive winner in the "Super Stars" contest. This outstanding athlete is first of all an outstanding Christian. He wrote a little book in which he declared that the central focus of his life is not soccer, the "Super Stars," football, basketball, or any sport. The real center of his life is his day-by-day relationship with Christ. He says, "I could do without any of the other things, but if I didn't have Christ, I couldn't function."

Paul would say that anything which prevents us from having a warm, personal, intimate relationship with Christ is a deficit no matter how desirous it may seem from a worldly standpoint. Furthermore, anything that we depend upon for our salvation other than Jesus Christ is a spiritual counterfeit. Perhaps the most difficult hurdle to get across in order to become a Christian is the idea that we find favor with God because of something we are, something we have, or something we do. These notions must all be flushed down the drain before we can have access to Christ.

Through much agony, Martin Luther had to discover this truth. He subjected himself to much physical and spiritual abuse in the effort to obtain peace of mind. He once said, "If any monk ever got to heaven upon his monkery, it would be I." Only when he discovered that righteousness was not something he attained by personal effort but gained through faith in Christ, was his spiritual quest resolved. The most persistent religious heresy is that salvation is a personal accomplishment. It violates man's pride to go to his knees in recognition of utter dependency upon the grace of God. When he recognizes that man is a "primordial stinker" rather than the captain of his soul, then he is ready to win Christ.

## Gaining Self-Fulfillment

Sacrificing our self-confidence in order to know Christ results in self-fulfillment. Christ delivers us from the crass aspects of our being and empowers us to live by the best that is within us. At last, we are on the road to fulfilling the destiny for which God designed us. The more completely we place our lives at the disposal of Christ, the more likely we are to be a good winner.

An article on the sports page of the newspaper said that in 1974 Rik Massengale's life was in shambles. He wasn't even making expenses as a touring golf pro. He was thinking about giving up golf and taking up farming. The game had become distasteful to him. Furthermore, his marriage was on the verge of rupture. His frustrations were reflecting themselves through an ulcer. He felt hostile and defeated. The article continued to say that a conversation with evangelist Billy Graham in a hotel room in Charlotte, North Carolina, changed all of that. Rik says that he entered into a personal relationship with Jesus Christ. Every aspect of his life improved. He began winning golf tournaments, and he declares that since entering into that personal relationship with Christ, he hasn't had a temper problem on the golf course. His marriage is good, and things are going right. He and his wife, Cindy, lead in a Bible study group on the pro golf tour.

The person who yields his life to Christ will be an attainer rather than a loser. In my counseling experiences as a pastor, I find that usually nothing much is wrong in most people's lives but that a commitment to Jesus Christ would straighten out. The unfortunate thing is that most people want to wish their troubles away or find simple solutions which they, themselves, can execute. They are unwilling to acknowledge that their problems are basically spiritual and that the answer lies in a closer walk with Jesus. Family tensions are usually indications of personality flaws and spiritual deficiencies. It takes better people to have better homes, and Christ is our principal resource in character enhancement.

Following Christ does not demand that we give up anything that is good for us. On the other hand, Christians avoid a lot of wear and tear in life because they avoid the rutty detours. Sometimes, people complain that Christians never have any fun. The fun thing, however, that would be denied to dedicated Christians often prove to be very volatile in wrecking lives.

Recently, a Texan was bitten by a pet rattlesnake which he had chosen to keep in a cage. In a moment of carelessness, however, he was struck by the reptile which he was keeping for fun. Drinking of alcoholic beverages, for example, is one of the fun things which many dedicated Christians deny themselves. Are they any worse for this deprivation? Many of their friends would say so, but, at the same time, cold statistics reveal that about one-tenth of those who indulge become alcoholics. The nonparticipant has thus avoided the unmitigated misery which snares the unwary drinker. Any honest evaluation of the dangers of alcohol will reveal that the Christian who disciplines himself to refrain from drinking is a winner rather than a loser.

## Playing to Win

Adela Rogers St. Johns tells of the time that her son, Dick, won the Metropolitan Boys' Tennis Championship. Bill Tilden, one of the greatest tennis players who ever lived, was coaching Dick and some other boys. In the car on the way home from a tournament, Tilden never said a word. This was more than Dick could stand, and he finally blurted out, "Hey, Bill, I won, didn't I? What more do you want?"

Tilden turned on the boy with cold fury and said, "You played not to lose. I saw you. Don't you ever dare as a Tilden pupil do that again. You will never get to the big time playing not to lose. You must always play to win." [1]

The person who gets to the big time in Christian living also must play to win. He is never satisfied with mediocrity. He aggressively goes after the prize. Here lies the secret between mediocre and victorious Christian living. Most Christians, it seems, are content not to lose. They are delighted that their souls have been saved. They rejoice in their spiritual security. At the same time, they relax into spiritual contentedness. There is no real thrust in their Christian life. They seldom exercise any initiative and never cultivate their potential. As a result, they never apprehend that for which they have been apprehended. In other words, they will never be all that Christ saved them for and wants them to be.

Paul was certainly one of the greatest Christians who ever lived. It is a bit disconcerting, then, to find him expressing such dissatisfaction with his Christian attainments. It is a fact, however, that the closer one walks with the Lord, the more conscious he is of his own inadequacies. I tried my hand at oil painting a few years ago and thought that some of my work was pretty good; that is until I compared it with the really proficient artists, then I hid my work away where no one would see it. When people have become satisfied with themselves as Christians, you can be sure that they have taken their eyes off Jesus.

The trouble is that far too many of us are content to be moderately Christian, relatively dedicated to Christ, and somewhat conscientious in our efforts to serve him. Churches today are only approximately fulfilling their mission because they are constituted largely of people who are comparatively Christian.

One of the reasons that Christians move in slow motion is that they are shackled by the past. In order to freely exercise his Christian gifts, Paul had some powerful forgetting to do. Paul had the blood of saints on his hands. He would have been completely incapacitated for Christian service if he had sat about morbidly reviewing those days in which he harassed the church. Could Paul ever tear from his mind that awful day when he watched over the cloaks of those who stoned Stephen to death? It was only by the grace of God that he could shut off the mental projector flashing scenes of past indiscretions upon the screen of his mind and get on with the business of serving Christ.

A man came to visit me one day who had been an infantryman in World War II. I had led him and his family to the Lord and baptized them sometime before. Yet, he had the spiritual impediment of not being able to forget the lives he had taken in battle. At times, he felt crushed by these reflections and considered himself completely unworthy to serve Christ. He was agonizing over the past for which God had forgiven him. Through prayer and counseling, he was finally able to close the door upon that dark memory and was later chosen as a deacon by his church.

On the Damascus Road, Christ gave Paul a new start in life. His past was buried under the blood of Christ, and it was very important for Paul by the help of the Lord to have a good forgetter. It is urgent not only to forget our past failures but also our past successes. Paul might easily have rested upon his laurels. He had strode across the Mediterranean world in seven-league boots, and wherever he stepped a church sprang up. He might have contented himself with his past accomplishments. We have a lot of spiritual retirees in our churches who stroke themselves with reflections of their past Christian service. They mentally tell themselves, "I've done my share. Now, I will leave it to the others."

Paul's letter to the Philippians is not a resignation but a recommitment. No one would have blamed Paul if he had written from his prison cell, "I have done all I can, and now it's up to you." We can easily lock ourselves in the cell of contentment and throw the key away, believing that no more could rightly be expected of us. Christ, however, talked about being faithful till the end. It was not until much later in his life when Paul sensed the end was at hand that he wrote his valedictory: "I have fought a good fight, I have finished my course, I have kept the faith" (2 Tim. 4:7). As long as there was life and opportunity, Paul kept pressing on. I believe it was the evangelist, Sam Jones, who used to say, "I'm going to bite the devil as long as I've got teeth, and then I'm going to gum him until I die."

One of the most remarkable men in our church is Charlie Bradshaw. This week, Charlie's picture appeared in our local newspaper with a lengthy article telling of his work in the Rotary International. Charlie conceived and initiated a program in the local club in which business and professional men would be asked to visit the high school classroom and tell the students about their work. This proved to be a valuable aid to students in the choice of their vocation. Charlie was asked to write a booklet describing the program, and it has been distributed to other Rotary Clubs throughout the nation. A few weeks ago, Charlie was asked to speak at the Rotary International Convention in San Francisco. Whenever I want a big job done in the church, I call on Charlie. He has looked upon his retirement years as allowing him more liberty to serve Christ and his community. He is an enthusiastic seventy-seven years of age and still pressing on. It has never occurred to Charlie to let up in his Christian service.

### The Prize Winner

Leo Durocher, the baseball mentor, once said, "Nice guys don't win ball games." I suppose it depends on what kind of a ball game you are talking about. In the race for economic wealth or the rough and tumble contest for political power, perhaps it is often the unscrupulous, the ruthless, and the tough who win. Paul was portraying the Christian life as a race in which all of us run and in which all of us may win the prize if we persist faithfully to the end. The prize in this instance is the commendation of our Lord Jesus Christ. In one of his parables, Jesus couched it in these words, "Well done, thou good and faithful servant" (Matt. 25:21). The good and the faithful are the prize winners in the kingdom of God.

Knute Rockne, the famous coach of Notre Dame, was once asked what he wanted most in a football player—weight, speed, or brains. He replied, "None of these. The desire to play football." What does it take to be a prize winner in Christian living—superior intelligence, outstanding talent, or educational degrees?

I think the primary quality for a Christian is that of a deep desire to live for Jesus. Unless we are driven by this desire, we can have all of these other qualities and still flunk out. This is not to discredit the importance of intelligence, talent, or education because Paul certainly was blessed with these things. If the burning desire is there, however, the Lord will take us with whatever natural endowments and make us champions. D. L. Moody was an uneducated shoe salesman whom the Lord used as the most dynamic evangelist of his day. In our time, in contrast, the Lord has taken a handsome, articulate, well-educated man named Billy Graham and used him to bless the world. The secret of their success is found in their overwhelming desire to magnify Christ.

Not only was there the desire to serve Christ but also to serve him in correspondence with his will. Paul was committed to the "high calling of God in Christ Jesus." The Lord Jesus Christ has a specific way in which he wants each of us to serve him. The prize winner is the one who diligently seeks to know the game plan and to obediently follow it. Roger Staubach is the popular and successful quarterback for the Dallas Cowboys football team. In an article in the *Guideposts Magazine,* he talked about his rough road to obedience.

It was a great day when Roger became number one quarterback for the Dallas team. Soon, however, he found himself chafing at the conditions. He was not allowed to call the plays; they were sent in by the coach, Tom Landry. He threw passes only when the coach said to and used running plays when the coach called for them. This was a real problem for Roger because his ego was involved. The implication of the situation was that Staubach was not good enough to know what plays to call. He went through a great spiritual struggle trying to accept the situation and to sort out the facts. Finally, he recognized how lucky he was to be the quarterback of such a football team. Furthermore, he was inexperienced and had a lot to learn about calling plays for the pros. His coach was one of the great minds of football strategy. He was finally able to accept the situation and led his team to victory.

The victorious Christian must let Jesus call the plays. He is the only one who knows the overall game plan. He is the great spiritual strategist, and he, alone, knows how he wants us to fit into his plan. This calls for frequent "skull practice" sessions with him in which we seek to absorb the game pattern and our part in it. We can be sure that if we obediently and enthusiastically follow his directions, he will lead us from victory unto victory. At the end of the season the prize will be ours.

### Notes

1. Adela Rogers St. Johns, *The Honeycomb* (Garden City, New York: Doubleday and Col, Inc., 1969), p. 22.

# 13

## Happy in Jesus

PHILIPPIANS 4:1-7,10-13,18-19

Happiness is the principal quest of life. This is demonstrated by the fact that we apply the happiness test to almost every venture of life. In reference to our vocations, we frequently ask each other, Are you happy in your work? as though happiness were the ultimate consideration in the worthwhileness of the task. Some persons flit from job to job seeking that elusive ingredient called happiness. There are people, however, who would not be happy with any work. They look upon work as a necessary evil in order to make a living and resent the demands of time and energy made upon them by any task. In contrast, someone has said, "Blessed is the man who has found his work. Let him ask for no greater happiness."

We also apply the happiness test to marriage, feeling that a happy marriage is a successful marriage. It may depend upon what it takes to make a person happy. If a man's happiness is dependent upon his wife remaining youthful and beautiful throughout their marriage or a woman's expectations that her husband will provide luxuriously for her comforts, then the happiness test is a very poor one. It would seem on the surface of things that when two people are genuinely in love, happiness would be the inevitable result of their marriage. Unfortunately, there are other ingredients that enter into marriage which sometimes destroy the happiness potential, such as selfishness, laziness, carelessness, and surliness; so we have the phenomenon of short marriages, quickie divorces, and sudden remarriages in which people are often surprised to find that the same old irritations exist in the new union.

Seldom do I ever talk to anyone who is blissfully happy in every area of life. Even casual conversations very quickly turn into gripe sessions in which people insist upon displaying their disappointments. We ordinarily interpret happiness to be that blissful state of affairs where everything is going our way.

Happiness is a job that doesn't require too much of us but pays a splendid salary; happiness is a wife who adores us and knocks herself out to please us; happiness is children who are mannerly and obedient; happiness is the bills all paid; happiness is plenty of time and money for recreation. It is not very realistic, however, to think that we can just roll merrily along through life without any hazards, heartaches, or hurts.

People who insist on living in a wishful world of everything just right are subjecting themselves to great disappointment and perhaps even an emotional crack-up. Ours is a world full of dangers, dilemmas, and difficulties. Does that mean that happiness is an impossible dream? *The Living Bible* translates verse 4, "Always be full of joy." [1] Is it possible every minute of our life to be 100 percent happy? Certainly not if our happiness depends upon circumstances.

Paul had some very harrowing experiences which you might like to review in 2 Corinthians 11:23–27. I doubt seriously if Paul was a laughing boy through the tortuous circumstances he lists there. Does happiness mean that we have to be always gay and giddy, or is it possible to be happy even when we are crying or sorrowing? The three little words which Paul appended to his instruction to rejoice may hold the clue. "Rejoice *in the Lord*" (v. 4, author's italics). He was talking about being happy in Jesus. The man who wrote these words was not living in an ivory palace at the moment where everything was convenient and luxurious. He was existing in the worst rat hole in Rome, a damp, dark dungeon. It is almost ridiculous to hear a man writing from a dungeon say, "Rejoice." Was Paul happy with this condition? He longed to be out preaching the gospel, visiting the churches, and advancing the kingdom. Imprisonment was a terrible frustration to this dynamic man. His happiness was in spite of his circumstances.

## Stick to Jesus

"Stand fast in the Lord" (v. 1), Paul admonished the Philippians. A person is on happiness ground when he maintains a vital relationship to Jesus Christ. It is Christ, not circumstances, who is the dispenser of the kind of happiness which endures. Happiness which can be destroyed with a phone call, happiness which fluctuates with the stock market, happiness which can be terminated with a doctor's report, happiness which shrivels when our children disappoint us is not substantial enough for me.

A book was published a few years ago entitled *If You Would Be Happy*. The author made the following statement: "Before we can be sure that religion brings happiness, we have to see that the great majority of religious people are happier week in and week out and all day long than a majority of agnostics and infidels. In my observation, this isn't so. Therefore, I must conclude that religion like all the rest of the lists we have gone through brings us many happy moments, but in most cases it can't be relied on through thick and thin." [2] Are Christian people no happier than other people? If the contention of this author applies to the Christian life, then the Bible promises are empty and Christianity is a fallacy.

Ethel Waters, who achieved fame as a singer and an actress, wrote a book entitled *To Me It's Wonderful*. She confessed that in her professional and personal life, she was never really happy or sure of herself. Her career of witnessing for Christ, however, she called "the gladest" thing she ever did. She professed to have been one of the devil's best customers but continued to say, "Some of the worst of us make the happiest Christians." The true secret of Christian happiness she discovered was in the commitment of her life to Christ. She said that she hadn't been displeasing him too much, but she really hadn't been pleasing him either.

Perhaps right here is a key to understanding why some Christians don't seem very happy. They are only half-heartedly living for Jesus. They are only Christian enough to make them miserable. They have not entered into the full joy of Christian commitment but are Christian enough that they can't really enjoy worldly things with a clear conscience. We must "stand fast in the Lord" if our happiness is to last. Faithfulness releases the joy of the Lord in our hearts. Don't expect to be happy in Jesus if you are out of Jesus.

## Gracious Toward Others

In order to be happy in Jesus, a close relationship with Christ is a necessity, but Paul continued to indicate that a compatible relationship with others is also needful. He prevailed upon Euodias and Syntyche to settle their difficulty and "be of the same mind in the Lord" (v. 2). Sometimes it is only "in the Lord" that people can get together. Even within the church, there are personality differences and incompatibilities which make it difficult to have a harmonious fellowship. When we commit these tensions to Christ, however, we can learn to love and appreciate each other in spite of the differences. *Today's English Version* translates verse 5, "Show a gentle attitude toward everyone." [3] Jesus Christ will remove the hostility from our hearts. This is one of the principal sources of our misery.

I heard about the man who went to the doctor because he had been bitten by a dog. It was discovered that the dog had rabies, and the man sat down and began to write furiously. The doctor advised him there was no need to write his will because he would pull him through safely. "Oh," said the man, "I'm not writing my will. I'm making a list of people I'm going to bite." Christ will take our enemies lists and tear them up. Christ will purge away our animosity, selfishness, jealousy, envy, and in their place bestow upon us love. Love is the happiness potion which fills our life with delight.

Malcolm Muggeridge has been for many years one of the most celebrated and scintillating British authors. In recent times, he has turned his life and his pen over to Jesus Christ. In his autobiography, he shares one of the great lessons of life: "All I can claim to have learnt from the years I have spent in this world is that the only happiness is love which is attained by giving, not receiving, and that the world itself only becomes the dear, inhabitable dwelling place it is when we who inhabit it know we are immigrants due when the time comes to fly away to other more commodious skies." [4]

His words remind us that Paul followed up his instruction about having a gentle attitude toward everyone with the announcement, "The Lord is at hand" (v. 5). Life is too short to spend it hating and begrudging and quarreling. We are all going to meet Jesus sooner than we expect, whether it be in his coming or our going. Why not spend these few brief years we have showering love upon others rather than projecting hostility toward them. Things would certainly be a lot more peaceful in our homes, in the church, and in the community. Furthermore, we, ourselves, would be a lot happier persons. Tolstoy once wrote in his diary, "The means to gain happiness is to throw out from oneself like a spider in all directions an adhesive web of love and to catch in it all that comes." [5]

## Don't Worry

How many times have you had those words addressed to you in an anxious moment? Now, Paul was saying to us, "Don't worry about anything." Is this realistic? A book was written a few years ago entitled *How to Stop Worrying and Start Living*. Do we have to wait until we have no worries before we can really live? We shall never be free of anxious and worrisome times, but it is important to turn these worries and anxieties over to the Lord. In that sense, we can learn to worry creatively. Our minds just insist on worrying. If we don't have any problems or worries of our own to occupy our minds, we will worry about somebody else's troubles. If we never worried, this would mean that we had no responsiblities and no relationships that really mattered.

Our worries communicate to us the fact that our existence makes a difference. But worry can be deadly and detrimental unless we learn to handle it in the Christian way. Smiley Blanton, a Christian psychiatrist, has said that anxiety kills more people than heart attacks or cancer. Dr. Charles Mayo has said that worry affects the circulation, the heart, the glands, the whole nervous system. "I have never known a man who died from overwork but many who died from doubt." Somehow, we must learn to cope with our worries, or they will destroy us.

I'm glad there is such a thing as worry. When I am sick, I want somebody to worry about me. I don't get any comfort out of the doctor shrugging his shoulders and saying, "Don't worry. You'll be all right. Just something going around." If somebody owes me some money, I would like for them to worry a little bit about it. I wish some of the people who take jobs in my church would worry a little more about their responsibilities.

Paul was suggesting a very positive action which will help us cope with our worries. We are to carry them to the Lord in prayer and let him help us handle them. Norman Vincent Peale has said that worry is a destructive process of occupying the mind with thoughts contrary to God's love and care. He offers the prescription for the cure of worry as that of filling the mind with thoughts of God's power, protection, and goodness.

## Accepting Life's Circumstance

One of the secrets of Paul's happiness was his ability in the Lord to adjust to the circumstances of life. Remember that Paul was a prisoner at the time he wrote these words. Could he really be content under those conditions to the extent that he did not beat his head against the wall and futilely rattle the prison bars? Instead of spending his days in miserable exasperation, he utilized them to write precious letters to the churches. It is too much to expect that life is always going to turn up roses. Everybody has good days and bad, happy times and sad. Unless we learn to take the vicissitudes of life in stride, there is no hope of happiness.

Contentedness is a rare quality, it seems. Seldom do we talk to anyone satisfied with their lot. We tend to be driven by a gnawing ambition, by a consummate pride, by a restless boredom. As somebody has said, "We not only want to keep up with the Joneses, we want to pass up the Joneses." Paul was a man who kept his wants under control. He said, "Neither do I speak in respect of want." His life was not controlled by his wants but by his love of Jesus and his compassion for souls. It would take more discipline than most of us possess to subdue our wants to the point that we could be content with little or much. If we have money, we are inclined to spend an inordinate amount upon frivolous things. If we do not have money, we are apt to spend our days envying those who do.

## Able for Anything

I like the way that Moffatt translates the thirteenth verse: "In Him who strengthens me, I am able for anything." [6] That's quite a boast. From anyone other than the apostle Paul, we might be offended by it. It would sound like pious bragging or even arrogance. Paul was not sipping tea in a comfortable parlor but was shackled in a Roman prison cell with every likelihood he would be executed. When a word like this comes from death row, it makes us sit up and listen. He was saying, "My ability to handle life's situations comes from the enabling power of Christ." Paul, then, was not bragging about his own prowess but confessing his weakness. He was saying that it is Christ who helped him overcome his own incompetency in the face of life's circumstances. Sir Harry Lauder, the great Scottish comedian, received the tragic news during World War I that his son had been killed. He later wrote that in a time like that there are three courses open to man. He may give up to despair, sour on the world and become a grouch; he may endeavor to drown his sorrow in drink or in a life of waywardness and wickedness; he may turn to God.

In 1948, Bobby Jones, the great golfer, suffered a spinal malady which crippled him. He had to become an observer of others playing the sport he loved so well. It must have been a terrible ordeal for him. He died not long ago and Ben Hogan, another notable golfer, said, "The secret is out, how Bobby

Jones was able to hold up. The secret was in the strength of his mind." There is some truth here. Bobby Jones had to be a strong-willed and strong-minded person to become the champion that he was. Three days before his death, however, he was baptized into the Roman Catholic Church. Even the great Bobby Jones must have felt that something was missing in his life.

A big, rawboned frontier wrestler and rail-splitter became president of the United States. Abraham Lincoln acknowledged, "I am driven to my knees in the realization I have nowhere else to turn." We should not be ashamed of our weakness. We are not gods but flesh and blood inhabitants of a world that is often cruel. We are subject to the sorrows, toils, and trials common to all men. This is the first step in unleashing in our lives the power of Christ.

Smiley Blanton, psychiatrist so long associated with Norman Vincent Peale, always kept a Bible on his desk. One patient remarked that he was surprised that a psychiatrist should have a Bible on his desk. He answered that he not only had it on his desk but also read it. "If a lot more American people would read their Bible, some of us psychiatrists could go fishing more often," he declared.

In his book *Inside the Third Reich,* Albert Speer, who was a close associate of Adolf Hitler, gives an interesting insight into the German pastor, Martin Niemoller. After the fall of Germany and Adolf Hitler's suicide, Speer, along with other Nazi leaders, was arrested and brought to trial at Nuremberg. Sunday services were offered for these former warlords, and Speer began to attend. He said, "The Sunday divine services were a great support for me." He tells us that of the twenty-six Nazis on trial, all except three attended the services.

One day, a bus drew up at the camp where Speer and the other Nazis were being held. It was rumored that it was a bus load of liberated concentration camp prisoners and that Martin Niemoller was among them. Niemoller had been a U-boat captain during World War I and later became the leading Protestant minister in Germany. Because he was an opponent of Adolf Hitler, he was thrown into the concentration camp and kept there throughout the war.

Speer had never seen Martin Niemoller, but among the new arrivals was a frail old man, white haired and wearing a black suit. Speer and one of his fellow prisoners decided that this was Niemoller. They felt sympathy for this man so visibly marked by years in the concentration camp. Speer's friend decided to go over and greet the broken man and express sympathy. When he addressed him by the name "Niemoller," the man immediately corrected him and said, "Niemoller is standing over there." Said Speer, "There he stood looking youthful and self-possessed, an extraordinary example of how the pressures of long imprisonment can be withstood." I am sure that Martin Niemoller would have said like the psalmist, "The Lord is the strength of my life" (27:1).

The Christian who depends upon the Lord can be happy and content because of the truth couched in verse 19: "My God shall supply all your need according to his riches in glory by Christ Jesus." God is not much concerned with our wants but is greatly moved by our needs. The way to be happy in Jesus is to live day by day in the awareness that the heavenly Father watches over you.

While attending the Southern Baptist Convention a few years ago, I met a friend from seminary days whom I had not seen for awhile. When I asked about his family, he said, "Well, I guess that since I saw you last we've lost our oldest boy. He was thirteen years old and died of leukemia just a few months ago." He said that it was only nine months from the time they discovered that the child was ill until he had died. But listen to his statement of faith: "You know, Vernon, we learned some things in this experience we would never have known otherwise. We learned that we had some resources available to us we had never really tapped." The Lord had seen them through.

Happiness is the supreme quest of every life. Happiness is the sure bequest of the heavenly Father to every person who abides in the Lord Jesus Christ.

## Notes

1. *The Living Bible.* Copyright © Tyndale House Publishers, Wheaton, Illinois 1971. Used by permission.

2. Ruth Stout, *If You Would Be Happy* (Garden City, New York: Doubleday and Co., Inc., 1962), p. 140.

3. This quotation is from *The Bible in Today's English Version.* Old Testament: Copyright © American Bible Society 1976. New Testament: Copyright © American Bible Society 1966, 1971, 1976. Used by permission.

4. Malcolm Muggeridge, *Chronicles of Wasted Time, Chronicle I: The Green Stick* (New York: William Morrow and Co., Inc., 1973).

5. Ralph G. Martin, *Jenny: The Life of Lady Randolph Churchill,* Vol. II, "The Dramatic Years" (Inglewood Cliffs, New Jersey: Prentice Hall, Inc., 1971), p. 4.

6. James Moffatt, *The Bible, a New Translation* (New York: Harper and Brothers Publishers, 1922).